The
SURVIVOR'S
JOURNAL

The
SURVIVOR'S
JOURNAL

A Woman's
Miraculous Journey

from Abuse to Freedom . . .
One Step at a Time

JEANNE JENSEN

A portion of the proceeds of this book will be used to support victims of domestic abuse.

Contents

Preface

I have opened up the pages of my private journal to share with you my hopes, my fears, and my personal experience as a victim of domestic abuse. The names and places have been changed. This is a true story. It's a story of faith and courage. It could be your story.

1

Thanksgiving Day

I had no idea that I was trapped inside an abusive relationship. I had always seen my marriage as an answer to prayer. The only troubling thing is that, looking back, I can see that my husband Frank had some anger issues and, strangely, he didn't travel well. Whenever we would go out of town for any length of time, there was always an explosion of anger some time during the trip.

My son Charlie was the first to notice it. In the early years, we would tolerate it. Frank would always apologize and say that his ears hurt from traveling or that he was tired or that he simply didn't understand what he was so angry about. Sometimes he would sleep the whole time that we were on vacation. After an outburst or episode of weird behavior, Frank would be sweet and promise to never do it again. And I would believe him. My son did not and for his twenty-first birthday, he begged me to visit him at college alone. I assured Charlie that I confronted Frank about his tendency to ruin every vacation and that he promised he wouldn't and was excited to come celebrate his birthday. We went and Frank ruined it.

The 2015 Thanksgiving trip to Greenville was the last trip that Frank would ever ruin for us. Once again, Charlie begged me to go to Greenville without Frank. I considered it. I was starting to take small trips without him. I had looked back over our eleven years of marriage, and I could not remember one trip that Frank hadn't acted out in some weird way or another. But I loved Frank. I believed him every time he was sorry and didn't know why he acted out in anger. Most of the time, he was a very fun-loving man, and I guess I just chose to hold on to those memories and forget the scary times.

That Thanksgiving Day was different. I had promised my son that my husband would not act out. When he did, I saw the whole situation from another perspective. I realized that something was really wrong. This was not normal and certainly not healthy.

We had just finished a beautiful dinner with our family. My sister and I were going to do the dishes and then just hang out and enjoy each other's company. I was out of cigarettes and getting anxious. Stupid habit. We both smoked. I asked Frank if he would run to the store to pick us up another pack. He took the car keys and left. After the dishes were done, we all gathered in the big living room and started chatting and laughing together like only family can.

I was standing in the middle of the room telling a funny story when Charlie ran in with his phone and said, "Mom, Frank is on the phone, and he's yelling at me. He said he's been trying to call you and you aren't answering."

I took Charlie's phone and said, "Hi Babe." And then Frank started cussing and yelling at me for not picking up my phone. I said, "You know I keep my ringer off and don't have it with me all the time. What's wrong?" He kept yelling and cussing, explaining to me that he was lost and couldn't find his way back to the house. I said, "Calm down. It's not a big deal. I'll get Mark on the phone, and he can tell you how to get back."

He wouldn't calm down. He continued to yell and freak out over the phone with Mark until he finally asked Frank to tell him where he was so he could meet him and have him follow him back to the house. After Mark hung up, he asked me what was happening.

I said, "I don't know. Apparently, he's overreacting." But I did know. This was all too familiar to Charlie and I. Frank was usually able to hide it from everyone else.

When Mark and Frank pulled up to the house, I was waiting in the driveway. I knew that I had to apologize for sending him out on this journey that triggered his anger. It was my fault. If I hadn't needed a cigarette, maybe this would never have happened. Frank jumped out of the car and ran up to me, shouting and cussing. He had that familiar "out of control" look in his eyes. It was very scary. He wouldn't listen to reason. I kept asking him to calm down, but he wouldn't. I guess Mark went into the house and told the family that Frank was really upset and that he was yelling at me. The next thing I saw was Charlie running out of the house with my mom and sister following behind. Charlie stepped right into Frank's face and told him to knock it off. They started cussing and yelling at each other while the rest of us looked on in amazement. None of us had ever seen this type of fight. This was the first time that Charlie ever raised his voice to Frank. Frank turned away and got back in the car and drove off. Charlie chased the car down the road with bare feet. We called for Charlie to come back, and he did. He was shaking with anger.

Everyone was asking me where Frank went and what was going on.

I said, "I don't know, but he has acted like this before. Why don't we all go back inside. He'll come back when he's cooled off."

He did come back, but he hadn't cooled off. I said, "Frank, let's go to the backyard and have a cigarette together. We need to calm down." He went to the backyard with me and we had a cigarette but he didn't calm down. I told him I was sorry for having him go out by himself, and I was sorry he got lost and I didn't pick up my phone. I told him he was scaring my family and then I said, "I knew you shouldn't have come."

He got so angry that he pulled back his fist to punch me, but he punched the fence behind me instead. My adrenaline went up. Frank had never hit me but had hit and kicked plenty of objects near me. I raised my voice and said, "You need to go home, and I'm not about to spend twelve hours in a car with you to get there! We can buy a plane ticket today and take you to the airport, and you will be home by tonight. Charlie and I can drive ourselves home in a couple days."

"I'm not getting on a plane."

"Fine, I'll buy a Greyhound ticket and put you on a bus."

"Rose, if you put me on a bus, I'll divorce you," he said.

That was the first time either of us ever said the "D" word. It was unthinkable to us. But at that moment I realized maybe our marriage wasn't as good as I thought it was. I knew my family was inside and very confused and worried. Maybe a good night's sleep would help everything to be better. He was refusing to leave, so I didn't know what else to do besides go forward. I went into the house and told my family that Frank just got upset because he got lost and that he would wind down. They weren't buying it.

"Everything will be okay; he just needs to wind down." I told Charlie and my mom to go back to my mom's house together and Frank and I would drive down by ourselves. Charlie came to me privately with my sister and begged me to not ride with Frank.

"It's not as bad as it looks. Frank always overreacts, and I'm used to it. He's not going to hurt me."

Charlie and my mom left. My sister Jo came to me crying. "I'm afraid of Frank," she said. "I've never seen him like this. His eyes aren't even focusing. I don't want him to kill you."

I assured her he wouldn't kill me and that I'd seen him like this before and he'd calm down. Before we left their house, Jo and Mark stopped Frank at the front door.

They said, "We're sorry this happened. We don't know what you're going through, but we want to know if you're okay."

Frank was much more passive and he said, "I'm sorry. I don't know what happened, and I'm sorry."

My sister Jo took Frank's face in her hands and said, "Look at me. I love you."

Frank started to cry, and so did Jo. They hugged and held each other for a while.

Mark looked at me with confusion and concern, and I said, "Everything's going to be okay."

We didn't say much on the drive to my mom's house. Frank went right to bed, and I knew I wouldn't see him until morning. My mom, Charlie, and I discussed the events, and I was actually happy that someone other than just Charlie and I witnessed this behavior. Charlie told my mom that Frank does something like this every time we travel, and then he's sorry and promises to never do it again—but he does. My mom was concerned about us traveling home the next day with Frank.

I said, "Well, he won't get on a bus or a plane, so I don't know what else to do."

Charlie said that he would drive the whole way home. We went to bed.

The next morning Frank got up and got his stuff together and said goodbye to my mom.

His demeanor was light and he seemed happy to be getting back on the road. He hugged my mom and told her that he loved her and thanked her for having us down. He didn't mention the events of the previous day. We got into our car and drove off. Charlie offered to drive, and Frank sat in the passenger's seat. I'd said that I wanted to sit in the back so I could nap. But really, I wanted to be able to see Charlie in the mirror. We gave each other strength. Frank was cheerful the whole way home. He never brought up the events of the previous day. He smiled, sang to himself, cracked a few jokes, and dozed off from time to time. Charlie and I kept occasional eye contact through the rearview mirror. I was sick to my stomach. I could play along with Frank's game and pretend that nothing bad had happened, but I was scared. A few times Frank offered to drive, but Charlie said he liked driving and would be okay with driving the whole way home.

It was a twelve-hour drive from Greenville back home to Madison. After nine hours, I was getting concerned for Charlie. I knew he was exhausted from yesterday's events, and so was I. I was too upset to drive. I would have trusted Frank to drive, but Charlie was having none of it. He was afraid that Frank would kill us. I just stayed quiet in the back seat. I was amazed at how Frank acted like nothing had happened. We were all supposed to just forget about it and move on. I joined in with Frank's fun conversation, but I could not just forget. I could not ignore my son's eyes in the rearview mirror. He looked tired, determined, and probably frustrated.

I said, "We need to stop and stay the night in Bristol. I don't feel well. We can all get a good night's sleep and drive the rest of the way home in the morning." Frank didn't argue, and we found a hotel just before midnight. When we got to the room, I said to Frank, "Why don't you just go to sleep? I want to take Charlie out for a beer. We will be back in an hour; I have my own key." Frank didn't argue. I didn't even wait for a response. I just said to Charlie, "Let's go," and we did.

We walked out of the hotel and down the street without speaking a word to each other. We turned the corner, and there were a few bars with people coming and going. I said, "Let's go have a beer together." We walked into the first bar on the street, sat down, and ordered a beer just in time for last call. I turned to Charlie and thanked him for driving all day. I told him I wanted to take him out to let him know I wasn't going to put up with Frank's behavior anymore. I had clarity. I was tired of playing games and tired of covering up for Frank's strange outbursts. It was nice to be out of the car and away from Frank. We looked around at the architecture of the downtown establishment and enjoyed our beer.

Charlie turned to me and told me something that would change the rest of my life. "Mom, I don't want to be like Frank. I know that he has been my dad for eleven years, but Jared was like a dad to me until I was ten. I want to be like Jared. But I will tell you that I have imitated some of Frank's behavior, and that led me to my first heartbreak. Danielle broke up with me because I didn't treat her right.

I want to tell you, coming from a man, that sometimes the best thing a woman can do is to tell a man who isn't treating her right that if he doesn't change his behavior, she will have to leave him."

I told Charlie that night I would confront Frank, but I wanted to do it my way. I would call the church and ask the pastor and his wife if Frank and I could meet with them so that I could confront him in front of some witnesses, and maybe we could just get marital counseling. I told him, "I promise you I will confront Frank, and I will no longer put up with this type of behavior."

I kept my promise.

2

Counseling

After we got home, things went back to normal. We both went to work and spent time together on the weekends, doing what we always did. Hiking, tinkering around the house, going to the movies. Things were different for me though. Frank seemed distant. We didn't talk much, and he was spending more and more time alone in the garage. He was always tinkering with something at the work bench. I didn't mind at all that he spent time alone in the garage. We had moved in with his mother because our finances got so out of control that we couldn't pay our rent. This was supposed to be temporary, but after two years, it was getting uncomfortable for everyone. But still, what was he working on? Whenever I would stop in to talk with him, it looked like he wasn't working on anything. Oh well, I was spending way too much time upstairs in our room watching *Cops*, so I figured he was just trying to hide from reality like I was.

Christmas was coming, and I wasn't looking forward to it. Everything was supposedly back to normal, but I could not shake the fear and helplessness I felt at Thanksgiving. I also felt an urgency to contact our pastor and his wife to ask for a meeting. If I didn't do this, time would go by, and I would assume everything was great until the next angry outburst. The last one was all too real in my memory, and I refused to sugarcoat it with the "everything is back to normal" facade. Besides, everything didn't seem normal at all.

I called the church and asked if Frank and I could come in for a meeting with Pastor Tim and his wife, Rebecca. I explained that I wanted to meet with both of them. Rebecca called me later, and I told her the whole Thanksgiving story. I told her I wanted to let Frank know I was afraid and that some things needed to change, or I would not be able to stay with him. She arranged for us to meet the following week. I told Frank I made an appointment for both of us to go in for counseling because of his anger problems and what happened at Thanksgiving. He agreed and said he would go. I was grateful.

The day we went in for counseling, I packed an overnight bag and put it in the back of my car before leaving for work. I really didn't know how the session would go, but I knew I had to be honest with Frank and tell him that if he didn't change his behavior, I would have to leave him. I had a fear that if I confronted him alone, he would deny it and get angry. I decided that if he got angry and had an outburst, I wouldn't go back home. I had no idea where I would go, but I packed a small bag anyway.

After work, I drove down to the church. Frank knew the appointment was at 5:30 and he was supposed to meet me there. He wasn't there when I arrived, so I walked inside and met with Tim and Rebecca.

Rebecca could see I was nervous. She patted my leg and said, "Can I make you a cup of hot tea?"

I said, "Yes," and as I sipped on the tea, I tried to relax. I sent Frank a text and asked him if he was coming to the church soon for our meeting.

He texted back saying, "Yes, but my car is broken down. I'm stuck at the grocery store parking lot, so if you want me to come, you need to come get me."

I felt very scared. I'm not sure what I was afraid of. I was starting to not believe everything Frank told me. Was he trying to trick me? Would I get there and have him shout at me about how upset he was that his truck broke down? This felt exactly like something that would cause him to overreact. And the thought scared me. I just sat in their office looking at the text.

Pastor Tim asked, "Is Frank coming?"

"Yes, but his truck broke down, and he said I would have to go pick him up."

"Where is he?"

"The Market on Fifth Street."

Pastor Tim stood up and said, "I'll go get him. I'll be right back."

By the time Frank and Pastor Tim arrived, I had calmed down sufficiently. And it seemed like the counseling session went well. Frank cried, we prayed, and we got some homework from Pastor Tim and Rebecca. My homework was to start attending a Tuesday night class on domestic abuse, taught by a woman named Cindy Sprague. She was the DA's assistant here in Madison. I didn't think I needed to go to a domestic abuse class, but I was willing to do whatever they suggested. Maybe I would learn how to help Frank with his anger. Frank's homework was to get together with either Pastor Tim or one of the other men in the church to just talk and pray. Pastor Tim gave Frank his personal cell phone number and said that they could get together just to fish or hike.

I attended the classes every Tuesday night from 5:30 to 6:30 p.m. Frank didn't seem to mind. After one of the classes, he asked me what the subject was that night. I said, "We learned about sociopaths, and I don't think you are one." He just shrugged it off and went back to his workbench. I thought for sure Frank would do his homework, but three months went by and he didn't call anyone.

I decided to keep a private journal. I bought a small red notebook that I could keep in my purse. Time was going by, and I didn't want to lose my focus. I felt like he wasn't treating me right, but I just couldn't put a finger on it. Maybe I was the problem? I felt like I was living in a fog.

Maybe writing down my thoughts in a notebook would help. Maybe writing down his strange behavior when I saw it would help. Make it more real. I felt like I was losing my mind.

I started becoming angry with my living situation. We'd been living with his mother for almost two years now. Our finances were hardly getting better, and I grew tired of sharing a household with my mother-in-law. I hated making a grocery list with her detailed instructions of exactly how big or small the sweet potatoes needed to be. I felt offended when she told me to take Frank with me to the store so he could pick out the meat. I was tired of hearing her complain about the smell of garlic cooking while I was making dinner. I began to hate having to turn on the fan while I cooked. One afternoon I came home with five bags full of easy meals from the grocery store. As I sat in the driveway, I memorized what I would say to her when I walked in. She would be where she always was, sitting on the sofa in the living room, watching TV. I was scared of her. Oh well, I was just starting to learn about personal boundaries from the Tuesday night classes, so I went for it.

"Patricia, I have decided that going forward it will be best for me if we buy our groceries separately and cook for ourselves individually. I've already told Frank and Charlie, and since we all have different work schedules, this will work best for me."

She turned her gaze from the TV to me, tilted her head down to look over her glasses and said, "Oh, really?!"

I said, "Yes," and walked out of the room. I felt good and bad at the same time. I realized that I had been growing distant in my heart to Frank and his mom. I didn't like this feeling. I loved them both, but I felt unappreciated.

I didn't know how long I should wait for Frank to keep up his end of the counseling homework. I had encouraged him a few times to call the pastor, but I didn't want to nag him. I was actually surprised he wasn't doing his part of the agreement. Life was back to normal alright. It was as if Thanksgiving had never happened—just like all the other times he acted out in anger. There was always an excuse, always an apology, always forgiveness.

Should I just forget about it and go on? That's what I had done for the last eleven years, but this time I couldn't. The Tuesday night classes were starting to bother me. I was starting to see that my husband was abusive. I knew he didn't mean to be, but his behavior fit the "cycle of abuse" pattern to a T. And my reaction was typical. I started to hate the classes. But I kept going. I cried through most of them and kept asking questions like, "Can the abuser change?"

3

The Call

I decided that I would just keep living "life as normal." I had the Tuesday night classes and my small red notebook to help me stay focused. I wasn't sure how long I was supposed to wait for Frank to keep up his end of the bargain of our counseling session. I just went to work, did errands, paid bills, and tried to be as pleasant as possible in my living situation. I even cooked a few meals for everyone. I was not thinking of divorce. I loved Frank and felt the Lord had brought him to me. He'd told me he had a difficult childhood, and he really wanted to go to an "anger management class." But in the eleven years we were together, he never did. He also wasn't reaching out to our pastor or any of the men our pastor suggested. I figured I would just wait. As long as life was back to normal and there were no anger outbursts, it wasn't so bad.

But something else was happening within me. I started to feel this pulling in my heart. It felt like God was calling out to me. It wasn't an audible voice, but a sense of urgency in my heart to reach out to God. I had felt this feeling many years ago in my youth, and I had responded. I was raised with a strong belief in God. It was evident to me that my mother knew the living God. She had a personal relationship with Him and seemed to love Him more than anything or anyone on this planet. She taught us about God and brought us to Sunday School to hear the Bible stories. At a young age, I asked Jesus to come into my heart. I wanted what she had—a relationship with God.

Jesus did come into my heart when I was a child. But as a teenager, I tried to push Him back out. He wouldn't leave. I did everything I could to run from Him, but He would not leave me alone. In my late twenties, I felt Him calling out to me. I felt like He wanted me to spend time with Him, praying, reading His Word, and fellowshipping with other believers. I didn't respond to His calling willingly.

I had trust issues, probably because my father left my mother for a younger woman when I was twelve. I'm sure that had something to do with it. I did not believe in love. I felt like love was the scariest thing in life. How could you surrender yourself to love someone fully if there was an outside chance they could "fall out of love" with you? I was angry with God for allowing my father to leave my mother and change my homelife. I went on a mission to break other hearts before mine could be broken, and I became very promiscuous.

It was at the end of my twenties that God stepped in. I had felt in my spirit that He was calling out to me to come back into fellowship with Him. I didn't want to. I didn't trust God any more than I trusted men. But He wouldn't let go. Finally, I gave up. My personal life was a web of twisted lies, and I was tired. I was living one life in front of my friends and family and a whole other life in secret. It was exhausting. I felt hopeless to change my behavior and started wanting to end my life.

But God stepped in. He had been calling out to me. He was still with me, and He saw through all my deceitful behavior. I was twenty-eight when I surrendered to Him, and He gave me the ability to walk away from my self-destructive lifestyle. But it was not without consequence. A few weeks after I walked away from that lifestyle and was rescued from suicide, I found out I was pregnant.

My brother Jared said that I should keep the baby, reasoning, "Rose, you have good intentions to live right, but maybe God allowed this baby to put a stake in the ground—something to keep you on the right track."

And he was right. I raised Charlie by myself although he was surrounded by loving friends and family. In a way, he was raised by "a village," a group of people who had all asked Jesus to come into their hearts. He was surrounded by people of faith.

I loved Charlie's childhood years. I wouldn't trade them for anything. But as he got older, I started to wonder if I was just being stubborn about remaining single. I prayed. In fact, when Charlie was nine, we both prayed together that the Lord would bring a man into our lives to be my husband and Charlie's father. It was Charlie's desire and mine. I promised the Lord I would cooperate with Him if He wanted me to be married. I fully trusted God.

Looking back, I still trust God. Frank was the man God brought to us, and we fell in love. I don't regret marrying Frank. I believe that "God works all things together for the good of those who love Him and are called according to His purposes." But now, after eleven years of marriage, I was starting to see a very scary pattern. I had heard that many people go through difficulties in marriage. That's why I sought counsel. I was doing everything I knew to do. So why was I starting to feel like God was calling out to me again? I hadn't left Him. Or had I?

Pastor Tim was one of my clients at the salon. The next time he came in for a haircut, I told him I felt like God was calling me. I told him I kept having this feeling like God was trying to get my attention, and I didn't know what He wanted. Pastor Tim asked me if I'd been reading my Bible. I said no, I hadn't read it for years. I felt like I'd been reading it all my life so I already knew what was in it. He told me that as a Christian, we need to spend daily time reading the Bible. He said that God speaks to us through His Word. He suggested I read just a little bit every day, like a vitamin. He said it would feed me, spiritually. I told him I thought that would be a good idea, and I would start doing that again. I remembered reading the Bible all the time in my youth. I had forgotten how wonderful it was.

I told Pastor Tim that except for neglecting daily Scripture reading, I wasn't really doing anything wrong. I asked, "Why do I feel like God is calling out to me? What does He want?"

"Maybe He wants you to go all in."

Go all in? What does that mean? I don't know how.

I told him I would think about that, and he told me he would be praying for me.

Another month went by. I had started reading my Bible again, and I was actually enjoying it. I had forgotten how much I loved the scriptures and how much I loved God. Frank and I had gone to church off and on during the last eleven years but were never really very involved. We would read the scriptures together in the early years, but Frank was unfamiliar with the passages and would not read on his own. I grew tired of reading to him, even though in the early years it was a very sweet time for me. I guess I wanted him to have his own relationship with God, personal and separate from our relationship with God together. I needed to have a private relationship with God, and I wanted him to have that too. Somehow, over the years, we managed to neglect a private or public relationship with God. Maybe Pastor Tim was right. Maybe I needed to "go all in," whatever that meant. I would think about it.

CHAPTER

The Texts

Three months had passed since Frank's Thanksgiving outburst. Things were back to normal. Well, the new normal of me not cooking and Frank and I not spending much time together. Even our conversations were full of "small talk." It almost felt like he was trying his hardest to never have another anger outburst so he could avoid his homework of meeting with one of the men at the church. I could tell he wanted all of this to get behind us so we could just go on with life. I was going on with life the best I could, but I had added the Tuesday night domestic abuse classes, as well as daily Scripture reading.

One evening after work, we decided to drive up to the woods to go for a hike together. We had left the driveway and were starting up the main road when Frank decided to answer a text while driving.

"Please don't text and drive," I said. "You know my son almost died because of that!"

He would not stop texting and was also cussing out the phone so, in my frustration, I grabbed his phone to see the all-important text. The text said, "Got those pills?" Frank's reply was, "I will get cash tomorrow."

It's hard to believe that the same person who spent her youth with serious trust issues could marry a man and trust him totally. But I was that person. From the beginning of our relationship, I felt our biggest strength was our ability to communicate with each other openly and honestly. He had always answered any question I would ask about his past, and I believed he was telling the truth. I never thought I'd have to look through my husband's phone. When we were first dating, he would constantly call or text to find out where I was or what I was doing. This bothered me, so I confronted him. He told me that in his past, he had trust issues because his first wife cheated on him; he left her and divorced her and thought he would never get married again. I promised him I would never cheat on him. To make him feel better, I told him that if I ever got tired of him or was thinking about cheating on him, I would just tell him up front and leave him. That way, he wouldn't have to worry about ever going through that kind of pain again. I meant that promise and never felt the desire to cheat on him. But seeing this text startled me. What a weird text. Is he buying or selling drugs? Is he using drugs? Could he be cheating on me? I never dreamed he would cheat on me.

I gave him back his phone and he said, "It's just stupid Tom." I didn't question him. Tom was one of his friends from childhood that I just would not keep a relationship with. He was an addict and was always in and out of serious drug use. I had told Frank when we first moved to Madison that he should no longer have anything to do with Tom. He was a bad influence. But Frank insisted on keeping the relationship. He said he keeps friends for life, no matter how screwed up their lives are.

I didn't want Frank to know how uncomfortable I was with the thought that he might be involved with drug use, so I just rolled down my window and talked about which trails we should hike and how much daylight we had left. But in my mind, I was concerned. Maybe he was hiding something from me. Maybe this was why he hadn't brought home a full week's pay since November. He hardly even worked all November and December. I decided that, for my safety, I was going to have to check his phone for more texts of this nature. I had never once thought about checking his texts. This was starting to feel like a nightmare. Thankfully, I had my "small red notebook" hidden in my purse. I had been writing down notes from the Tuesday night classes. I would write down a note about this text. I didn't want drug use to become a new normal.

The hike was different than our usual hikes together. There was a thickness in the air. Frank kept wandering off ahead of me and looking into the plants and rocks along the trails. He hardly talked with me. At one point, he went several yards ahead of me and down into a ravine. I called out to him to wait up for me. What was he looking for? It felt almost exactly like his behavior in the garage. Totally distracted and yet focused on insignificant items. I was distracted too. I felt he must be hiding something from me, and that made me feel unsafe. Tomorrow, I would check his phone and make notes of the texts if any of them seemed unusual. I would keep track by writing the texts in my small red notebook.

The next night, Frank came home late, even though he said he could get off work at any time. He didn't want to go out hiking again. He went upstairs to take a shower. I noticed that he left his phone in the garage, so I risked looking at his texts. He got a text from someone named Sally.

> **SMALL RED NOTEBOOK:**
> Sally: "I like you 1, 2 & 3 :)"
> Frank: "Keep lovin me yo!"
> Sally: "Oh yeah!"

What does that mean? Who's Sally?!! Oh boy . . . don't jump to conclusions. I've got to stay calm. There was another text.

> **SMALL RED NOTEBOOK:**
> Sally: "Cause he has been keeping my son company and besides that, he has worked every day."

I think he might be cheating on me. I can't breathe. Maybe I am imagining all of this. There's got to be a rational explanation. Maybe the next text will make things more clear.

SMALL RED NOTEBOOK:
Sally: pic text (erased)

Oh my gosh . . . it's so sad. Lord, I trusted you. I even trusted you with my son! This would make me sick and break my heart. If I find out Frank is really cheating on me, I will ask Pastor Tim and Mark Rizzo to help. I'll ask my family to help my son and me to get out safely. My trust in Frank would be forever broken.

5

The Plan

After class on Tuesday, I told Cindy about the texts. "I think that Frank might be using drugs, and I think he's cheating on me. He lies a lot, and I don't trust him, and I don't know what to do."

She suggested I lay low and try to go moment by moment, while calmly and prayerfully making a plan to leave him. She said, "Your truth is your truth."

I was quite sure Frank was cheating on me and using drugs. She said he would deny it and get angry so I didn't need to bother confronting him. She suggested I get Charlie out of the house and into a safe place. I asked, "What will I say to Frank after I leave him and he asks why?"

"You could say, 'I think you know, Frank.'"

It sounded like such a simple plan, but it felt like it was going to be the scariest, most difficult thing I'd ever done.

I felt overwhelmed. I decided to write her plan down in my small red notebook.

> **SMALL RED NOTEBOOK:**
> The next step
> Lay low
> Go on moment by moment
> Eat, drink, sleep, be happy, work and get rest
> Let Charlie know that I'm planning to leave Frank
> Follow God's leading

The next day, I sent Frank a text that said, "Love you." There was no response for a few hours. When he did reply, he sent a text that said, "Reset my phone to factory. Reset acting weird. Call when you can." It felt like maybe he was trying to erase all his texts. Was he on to me checking his phone?

Pastor Tim came in for a haircut that day, so I told him everything that had been going on since our counseling session. He seemed burdened. He looked disappointed and maybe even a little angry. He told me to get out of the house as soon as I could. He suggested I go to a friend's house or to a safe house or even find a one-bedroom apartment. "After you leave Frank, he needs to stay away from you and not even talk with you unless he shows true repentance. Frank needs to have stopped using all drugs, including pot. And don't go back to him until he is getting help, has a two-bedroom apartment for you to live in, and has a real job or two jobs!" He told me I had to confront Frank—not in a condemning or judgmental way, as if there were no hope for repentance, but in a way that showed his behavior was intolerable. "You cannot live in that environment," he said.

It was going to be impossible to find a one-bedroom apartment in this town. I had just read in the paper that Madison was experiencing a housing crisis. The rental vacancy rate was at 2 percent. It would take a miracle. My heart was starting to break. It would have seemed easier to just believe the lies and pretend that none of this was really happening. But I wouldn't let myself. I had made a promise to Charlie, and I was seeing things very clearly for the first time ever. And God was still calling out to me. I felt His presence very close. I felt like I had to follow the advice I was given and make a plan to get out. I could not simply confront Frank and say, "Hey, I saw some texts . . . who's Sally?" I had seen the way he reacted to confrontation. It was never his fault, he was the victim, I was imagining it. I couldn't afford to let myself get tangled up in his deceit. I couldn't even allow myself to realize that once I walked out, the marriage would end. I let myself hope that Frank would admit to being untruthful with me. I let myself hope the marriage could be saved. I decided to follow Cindy's advice and go moment by moment. I called her and told her I was afraid and that this plan seemed impossible.

She said, "God will open a window of opportunity."

I chose to believe her.

CHAPTER

The Cost

I can understand why so many people stay in unhealthy relationships. You become inter-twined with each other's friends and family members. You hope against hope that things aren't so bad. You go to counseling and work hard to keep a good attitude, just in case the problems are your fault. Sometimes the problems are so vague that you don't even realize there is a problem. And you search within to see if maybe you are the problem. "Abuse" is a word that is thrown around a lot in our society. Some people endure physical abuse, and some people endure psychological abuse. I have come to believe that something as overlooked as the lack of respect for another human being should fall into the category of abuse. It is cruel to deceive those who trust you.

I have authority on this issue because I spent seven years of my youth living a dual life. And when I came clean, I hurt those who loved me the most and trusted me. I know that the journey of life can be a very real struggle at times. And each person has their own level of tolerance. But when it comes to love and marriage, there must be respect. And trust.

I could no longer trust Frank when I found out that, besides lying to me and secretly using drugs, he was having an affair with another woman. And because of his tendency to have angry outbursts, I was fearful. Sometimes when he was angry, he would go off on a rant saying things like, "Oh man, I'm gonna kill somebody!"

The Tuesday night domestic abuse classes, along with my own gut-instinct, told me to get out of that relationship and out of that house as soon as possible. But how? We had a storage unit in town where we were storing the entire contents of our home. We filled it up when we moved in with Frank's mother. It was supposed to be temporary until we could get our finances in order. I decided to use the storage unit for my advantage. Yes, I could just walk out and leave my belongings behind, but Cindy had told me not to panic. Her advice of "going moment by moment" was the only thing that kept me from panicking. Every evening after work, I would load some of my personal belongings into my car and drive into town to put them into the storage unit. It seemed the responsible thing to do.

Cindy's advice to me was to "keep playing the game one day at a time." She said, "Don't get freaked out about playing the game. Be as loving as possible. It's okay, you just do it. Lay low, stay calm, and take one day at a time." She knew I was struggling with being dishonest with Frank. She encouraged me that I hadn't done anything wrong and said, "This is God's will for you right now."

After one of the classes, I told Cindy that I was starting to panic. I pulled out my small red notebook and said, "Tell me what to do." Cindy's advice was straightforward. She didn't complicate things, so I wrote it down.

> **SMALL RED NOTEBOOK:**
> 1) Get an apartment
> 2) Get a restraining order
> 3) Get out

It sounded so simple. And so scary. Would I be able to find an apartment? Did I have the courage to put a restraining order on him? I knew how I would be perceived by his friends and family. Was it worth it? I knew I would possibly have to leave some of my personal possessions behind, including my pets. The cost to consider was huge. I didn't know if I could do it.

I decided to keep moving forward, one moment at a time. I was in a hard place, and I had some big decisions to make, but I knew I was not alone. God was still pulling at my heart. I felt that He was with me. I did not want any of this to be happening, but it was. So I chose to trust God. The plan sounded so simple, but I had to count the cost. Could I do it? Could I afford not to?

7

Shooting Star

The feeling that God was calling out to me continued. I had started reading my Bible a little bit every day, as Pastor Tim had suggested, but I still didn't really know why God was calling me or what He wanted me to do. I continued trying to live "life as normal" while privately working on a plan to get out safely. No one but Cindy knew about my plan. Somehow, I was still able to function at work.

I enjoyed the appointments with my clients who had a relationship with God. I told one of my clients, Stan, that I felt like the Lord had been calling out to me but I didn't know what He wanted.

Stan told me that there is a verse in the Bible that says, "Draw near to God and He will draw near to you." And he told me that he would be praying for me. This encouraged me to keep praying, reading my Bible, and asking God how to "go all in."

Another client, Anna, came in and I told her that I rarely watch TV. She asked me why, and I told her it hurt me to see filth and indecency on TV and film. Anna told me that maybe I am "marked by God." She said that in the Bible, Isaiah talks about people who were grieved by sin around them. She said those people were "marked by God."

Hearing these encouragements from my clients was humbling to me. I decided that I would cooperate with God. I would let Him be my God and my Lord. I wanted to "go all in."

A few nights later, I was fast asleep when, all of a sudden, I was startled by a dream or a voice that said, "Talitha cumi." I sat up, wide awake. I looked at the clock and it was 3:00 a.m. I just sat there thinking for a minute. How weird. "Talitha Cumi." I know what that means. They were the words Jesus spoke to the little girl who had died. They were the words He spoke while holding her dead hand. They were the words that brought her back to life. The words "talitha cumi" mean, "Little girl, I say to you, arise."

I got out of bed and walked down the stairs. My dog Lady followed me. I wanted to go outside to have a talk with God. I stepped outside and stood next to the garage. It was dark and cold. I looked up into the night sky. The stars were brighter than usual. I forgot that stars do sometimes twinkle. The black silhouette of the pine trees only enhanced the beauty of the night sky. I felt like I was looking into the universe.

I thought, *Well, I'm just going to look up at the stars and talk to God. I know He's out there. Maybe He will be listening from behind the stars.* Before I could even say a word, I started to cry. The nightmare of my crumbling marriage flooded my thoughts. I just stood there in the cold, looking up into the sky. I couldn't pray yet. I was thinking, *This is a nightmare. Why is this happening to me? I don't know if I can go on.* I felt like I had been betrayed by my husband. I had trusted him with my heart and my body. This betrayal was sickening, and I felt afraid. The last few days had been so hard for me. I knew my husband was involved with another woman. I was quite sure he was using meth or some other drug besides the daily pot smoking. But I was afraid to confront him. He would probably lie about it all and get angry. I could not allow myself to be the object of his outrage.

I just stood there, looking up into the starry sky. I was trying to gather the courage to pray to a God who was allowing me to go through such a difficult situation. Just then, I remembered a painting I had seen as a child of "Daniel in the Lions' Den." I closed my eyes and I could see it in my mind. Daniel was standing on the floor of a lion's den. He was wearing a robe and tunic, and his hands were folded in front of him. His head was tilted up, and he had a peaceful look on his face. Large lions surrounded him in the shadows, some standing, some walking, and some lying down. But all of the lions' mouths were closed, and they were not hurting Daniel. I thought about this painting as I gazed into the night sky. I thought, *Daniel was not afraid. He did not waste his energy questioning why God had allowed him to be thrown into a lion's den. He just stood there and patiently waited for God's next move.* His faith and absolute trust in God encouraged me.

I thought, *God brought Daniel and many other people through impossible difficulties. I'm going to trust that God will deliver me safely out of mine.* I stood there quietly and tilted my face to the night sky. I said, "Lord, I feel like Daniel in the lions' den. I see danger all around me and no safe way out. I don't want to be afraid; I want to trust you. I want to 'go all in' but I don't know how. Lord, I give up. Please help me. I can't navigate this life without your help. It's too hard for me. I've never been any good at directions. I don't know where you are or what you want, but I know there's no hope for me without you. I want to stop trying and just surrender to you. I give up, Lord; I want to let go. Please help me."

As I finished my prayer, with tears streaming down my face, I saw the fattest shooting star I have ever seen. For a minute I thought, *Thanks for the shooting star, God, but I still don't know how to go all in.* Then I thought, *No, that was awesome! A shooting star, just for me!! Thank you, God.*

When I got back into bed, I laid down and thought of an idea. I would ask Pastor Tim if I could be baptized again. Easter Sunday was coming up, and I knew they were going to have a time for baptism after the service. Even though I had been baptized years ago, maybe I could show myself and God that I was "going all in" by going under the waters of baptism again. I wanted to finally let go completely and let God be sovereign. I wanted to lay under that body of water and die to my own efforts. And I decided that when I would come up out of those waters, I would step out in absolute trust that the God who made me and loves me was willing and able to navigate me through the rest of my life.

CHAPTER

Easter Sunday

It was Easter Sunday, the day I had been waiting for. Green Valley Church combines all three services into one large event on Easter morning. They hold the service in an open-air amphitheater in the middle of downtown Madison. It's always exciting! Everyone brings their own lawn chairs or blankets, and the grassy area fills up fast. Everyone else sits on the cement planter boxes or on the stairs leading down to the theater. The worship band sets up on the stage, and their music is heard for blocks. There's a portable baptismal pool that they set up at the edge of the stage for anyone who wants to get baptized after the service.

I had told Frank I wanted to get baptized this Easter. I explained I felt like God was calling out to me, and I wanted to respond by "going all in" and being baptized again. Frank's twin brother Richard and his wife Janice were in town with their three kids. They arrived the night before to spend Easter weekend with Patricia and us. It was always a challenge when anyone came to Patricia's house because we were renting two rooms from her, and it was a three-bedroom house. Charlie was always willing to spend the night at a friend's house or sleep on the sofa when she had company. His room became the guest room. Frank never minded having family over for a visit. It was I who didn't like to have company forced upon me. But it was Patricia's house, not mine, and she had the right to have her children and grandchildren over anytime she wanted! I just hated the fact that we were living with my mother-in-law. I was working hard to get our finances on track so we could move out.

I woke up early and got ready for church. I chose a tan pair of lightweight pants and a grey T-shirt with white trim. No make-up, nothing fancy. I dressed to get baptized. I packed a pair of sweatpants and a hoodie in my backpack to change into after the service. It was a cold morning. Even though it was Easter, spring had not quite yet come to our valley. I could hear that Richard and Janice were already up with the kids opening their Easter baskets. I went downstairs to get a cup of coffee and to enjoy the kids for a few minutes. Frank came down to get some coffee and then went outside with Richard to smoke a cigarette. He looked handsome in his white long-sleeved shirt and grey slacks.

I went out to let Frank know that I was ready to go. He seemed agitated. I asked him if he would rather stay home with his family. I told him I wouldn't mind going alone since I was only going to get baptized. He said he was only going to go because he thought that I wanted him to go with me. I told him, "If you don't mind, I would actually rather go alone. This is something I feel I have to do, and it is very personal. I don't mind going alone." He asked if I was sure and I said, "Yes, I'm sure. Go inside and enjoy your family. I'll be back in time to help with the Easter dinner. We'll have a nice afternoon with your family." He gave me a kiss and a hug and thanked me. I thanked him and drove down the driveway. I was actually relieved to be going to church alone this Easter.

It was strange walking up to the service by myself. The sun was shining, but the air was cold. I noticed families walking up the sidewalk, dressed in their Easter outfits, and here I was wearing pants and a T-shirt and carrying a backpack. I didn't care. I came for one reason only—to "go all in" and to prove it to myself by being baptized. I found a corner of one of the cement planter boxes near the stage, and I sat down. Worship was beautiful. I felt like I was dreaming. Pastor Tim preached a sermon about how amazing Jesus is. He ended it shouting facts about who Jesus is and what He has done and what He is going to do. It was stirring, and I felt myself not caring about who I was or wasn't. It was all about who Jesus is.

As soon as the invitation to be baptized was offered, I was in line. I felt myself trembling. It was from the cold and from fear. I was terrified. I was afraid of really "going all in" for Jesus, and I was afraid of my current situation. What was happening in my marriage? Was Frank really cheating on me? Was he doing drugs? Was I in danger? One of the attendants asked me how I was doing and if I had any questions about baptism. I assured her that I totally understood what I was about to do and thanked her for asking.

I could hardly breathe before my turn to step into the pool. I saw Pastor Tim standing in the water. He held up his arm to help me in. I smiled and stepped into the pool. He smiled back at me with the kindest smile. I said, "I'm ready to go all in." He asked me to cross my arms over my chest, and he held my hand and my head as he prayed a beautiful prayer over me. I was still trembling, and I could feel tears streaming down my face. I wasn't sure why I was crying. Maybe it was because of all the fear.

I will never forget the feeling I had once I was fully submerged in the water. I felt like I was dying to myself. I was dying to my abilities and my inabilities. I was dying to my fears. I was going all in and joining Jesus in His death for me. While I was under the water, I thought to myself, *When I rise out of these waters, I will rise with Christ! I have surrendered my life to Him, and I will rise in His strength and power, not mine.*

When Pastor Tim pulled me up from the water, he said, "God's callings are irrevocable. Now go and live it!" I climbed the steps out of the baptismal pool and someone gave me a towel and a Bible. I said, "Give the Bible to someone else. I already have one." Then I walked to the back of the stage and saw Preston Warner. He is one of the associate pastors at Green Valley, and I had gotten to know him from the finance class I had taken at the church a year ago. I said, "Hey, Preston, can I tell you something?"

He smiled and said, "Sure Rose."

"This is strange, but I'm not shaking." I held out my hand, and it was calm. I was standing straight, and my entire being was calm. Inside and out. Even though it was cold, I was calm. Even though I was heading right into the middle of an emotional storm, I was perfectly calm.

He said, "Isn't God awesome?"

"Oh yes!" And then I said, "Where can I change?" He pointed to a building across the street and told me that the owners of the business were letting us use their restrooms to change clothes after the baptisms. I thanked him and hugged him and walked across the street to change my clothes. While I was walking, I was still amazed at how calm I felt. I was happy to finally let go of everything. I felt courage and confidence. God was with me. God was in control.

9

Spring Cleaning

I didn't understand why all this was happening to me, but I knew that God understood and that He was in control. I decided to stop bothering with fear. I was just going to move forward, trusting that God would go before me. I had been looking through the newspapers and the internet, searching for an apartment or small house to rent, but there were very few homes available. Our town was experiencing an all-time-low vacancy rate. Both my pastor and Cindy had advised me to separate from my husband. I'm not sure how other people separate in their marriages, but it seemed impossible for me to simply talk with Frank about it. I was concerned for my safety. I did not want to fight or argue with him, and I did not want to watch him lie to my face. I had this feeling that he would accuse me of imagining all of it. I no longer trusted him and feared that he might hurt me. I wanted to get out safely, put a restraining order on him, and then work it out from a distance.

But where could I go? I could go back home to Greenville and stay with any one of my family members, but then I would lose my job. I didn't want to leave Madison just yet. I felt that if I ran away from Madison, I would end up hating Madison and even being afraid of Madison. The city didn't do anything wrong. It felt best to find a place in town. Maybe Frank would change his behavior and we could be reconciled.

On my lunch break, I walked into a realtor's office. I looked around and found some forms to fill out in order to get on a waiting list for an available apartment in town. As I sat down to fill out the application, I realized I couldn't put Frank's information or my current landlord's information because my current landlord was Frank's mom! This whole process of "getting an apartment, getting a restraining order, and getting out" was impossible. I filled out what I could on the application and walked up to the desk.

A nice woman named Judy smiled at me and said, "May I help you?"

"Yes, please. I am looking for a one-bedroom apartment in town. I don't care where it is, but it needs to be under $1,000 a month."

She asked if I had filled out an application.

I said, "Yes, but I can't give you any information about my husband because I'm planning to leave him, and I don't want him to be able to find me."

She looked me in the eyes, held out her hand for the application, and asked, "Are you safe?"

"Yes," I said, "but I don't feel safe confronting my husband."

She took the application and started entering my information into her computer. "Here's the thing," she said. "We have a waiting list for apartments in town right now, but I'm going to move you up to the top of the list. I have experienced the same thing you are going through right now, and I will do what I can to get you into an apartment as soon as one becomes available."

I sighed and smiled and said, "Thank you so much."

When I got home from work that evening, I looked around at my belongings. I started to visualize how much time it would take to gather everything and get out quickly. It would not be possible to get out quickly, and Frank's mother rarely left the house. I decided to do a "spring cleaning." I would start with my desk. I would go through each drawer and throw away what I no longer needed. I could put all of my important documents into one container. Then there was the closet. I would go through each piece of clothing and get rid of what I didn't wear. But what about my Kitchen-Aid? I loved to bake, and this was a gift from my mother years ago. I felt overwhelmed.

My courage and determination to get out came later that evening. While Frank was in the shower, I checked his phone for texts. There was a recent one from Sally!

Frank: "I'm sorry, Sally, but I won't be able to come over tonight. My car is running like crap."

Sally: "It's ok, I understand."

I went to bed and just laid there. My thoughts were spinning. *This has been too much for me. I can't eat, I dream about tidal waves, and my body feels like it's been through a train wreck.* But guess what? When I was ignorant and innocently trusting my husband, I slept well, ate well, and was able to digest my food. I laid there and told myself, *Frank is only a man. I can trust God. I can relax and breathe and smile. I can trust my Savior.*

The next morning, I got a call from Judy at the realtor's office. She told me that I was the first in line for an apartment that had on-site security. She said it might be available next week. I knew I needed to stay alert and be ready to leave.

I decided it was time to tell Charlie I was planning to leave Frank. One night, just before going to bed, I went into Charlie's room and said, "Charlie, I need to tell you something." He looked concerned. I said, "Remember after Frank's outrage at Thanksgiving, how I promised you that I wouldn't put up with it anymore?"

"Yeah." I could see fear and concern in his eyes.

"Well, we had a counseling session with Pastor Tim and Rebecca. I was sent to a class on domestic abuse, and Frank was told to meet with Pastor Tim or one of the other leaders in the church. I have done my part, but Frank has done nothing. I've been advised to get out. And I've been moving all of my stuff into storage and looking for an apartment to rent."

Charlie whispered, "What if Frank tries to kill us? I don't want to die."

"Well, I don't think that Frank would try to kill us," I said, "but I am planning to put a restraining order on him, which will mean that he can't come near me for a year unless he wants to go to jail."

"I'm scared," Charlie said. "How are you going to do it?"

"I'm not really sure. I'm just taking one step at a time and trusting God. I can't afford to be afraid right now, and neither can you. We have to believe that God is guiding us and He will protect us. You should start taking stuff out of your room so we can be ready to leave quickly when the time is right."

"Okay" he agreed. "I'll ask Chris if I can store some of my stuff in his room."

I spent that weekend "spring cleaning" the room, the closet, the office area, and the garage. Since we had the entire contents of our last home locked up in a storage unit downtown, I decided to tell Frank I was feeling a little cluttered at his mom's house and that I wanted to put some of our stuff back into storage until we could move out. I took three carloads of our belongings down to the storage unit. I was moving fast. I wanted to be ready to go when the door opened up for me. It felt strange to lie to Frank. It wasn't my custom to lie. In fact, I hate lies. But I was grateful for Cindy's advice to me. She told me, "Right now, you need to play the game. I know that as a Christian it feels wrong to lie, but right now you need to lie to get out safely. This is God's will for you right now."

That Sunday evening, I was tired. I decided to clean the house and wash Patricia's wood floors one last time. I wasn't sure when or how I would leave, but it was just something that I wanted to do. I also decided to make a nice dinner for everyone. I felt good about all the hard work I had done over the weekend. It felt good to get some of my belongings out of the house and into our storage unit. I knew that when I left, I would leave much behind and I had the feeling I would never go back. It was difficult emotionally, but I felt a sense of urgency.

The evening sun was shining into the kitchen as I finished preparing dinner. The house was quiet. I remember how pretty the wood floors looked in the sunshine. I felt sad. I didn't want to leave Frank. I loved him. Frank walked into the kitchen and gave me a hug. I held him and said, "I love you."

He kept hugging me and said, "The house feels so good and clean. It feels like we're moving out, but I know that we're not moving out." Frank has always been so intuitive. I wished I could have just talked with him and told him that I knew he was cheating on me. I wished I could have asked him if he was doing drugs. I wished he could be honest with me, but I didn't know if he could, and I couldn't afford to experience another one of his anger explosions. We just stood there in the kitchen hugging. Time stood still. Then Frank said, "It feels like you're leaving me."

I said, "I would never leave you, Frank."

10

The Exit

The next morning, I woke up early and felt refreshed. I got some coffee and talked with Frank while he got ready for work. It felt good to have the house clean and all of my important belongings safely in the storage unit downtown. I kissed Frank goodbye as he left for work and said, "Have a good day! I'll see you at 4:30."

I walked back into the kitchen to get another cup of coffee. The house was quiet. It was my day off, but I woke up earlier than usual. Everyone was still asleep. I walked past Patricia's room on my way upstairs and thought to myself, *I can't believe she's still asleep. She's usually up by now, drinking her coffee and watching TV.* When I got to my bedroom, I looked around and saw everything clean and organized. I took a minute to visualize how long it would take to get all of my items downstairs and into my car. I thought, *It will take about four trips up and down the stairs.* I stood there thinking, *This might be my window of opportunity. Patricia never sleeps in.* I knew that the time to get out was now.

I opened up Charlie's bedroom door, and he was just getting up. I walked over to him and whispered, "It's time to go now. Patricia is sound asleep, and Frank has left for work. Now is the time. Gather as much as you can and load up your car."

"How are we going to do it? What if Grandma wakes up?" he asked.

"I don't know. I feel like this is the time. Maybe God is keeping Patricia in a deep sleep for us to get out."

"I can't fit everything into my car," he said.

"I'm planning to move very quietly and very quickly. I'm not going to be able to get everything out either, but we'll get what we can. It's all just stuff, and now is the time to get out. You can put some of your things into my car too. Just move fast. Let's go!"

The next twenty minutes were surreal. Quietly, Charlie and I passed each other on the stairs, our arms full of clothing. Quietly, we passed each other as we walked through the garage to our cars, parked on the driveway with the doors and trunks open. Up and down we went, gathering our most important belongings. I paused by the kitchen and thought of all my items that were now shared property with my mother-in-law. I had to leave it all. I knew that I was running out of time. Patricia was still asleep, and I sure did not want to have to explain to her why I was sneaking out of my home. I went upstairs one last time. I looked at my cuckoo clock on the wall. I'd have to leave it. I had already loaded up my car with clothes, toiletries, my jewelry box, and everything from my desk. There was a small chest of drawers that had more of my jewelry and some sentimental items. I had always liked that piece of furniture. It wasn't too big to carry downstairs, so I decided it would be the last thing I would take out.

Charlie walked into my room and said, "Mom, I'm not going to be able to take everything out of my room. I think we should go. What if Patricia wakes up?"

"Okay, this small chest is the last thing I'm going to take," I said. I lifted it up, and all the items inside shifted and made a noise. I put it back on the floor and looked at Charlie. I whispered, "Let's go!" As we started to leave the room, we both noticed our dog Lady, sprawled across the bed, sound asleep. She never sleeps when any of us are awake. I thought, *The Lord must have put a deep sleep on her too.* Charlie and I paused long enough to give Lady a scratch on the head and a kiss. We didn't have time to be sad. We looked at each other and smiled. We both gave Lady another kiss and left.

When we got outside, Charlie said, "Where are you going to go?"

"I don't know,' I said. "First, I'm going to go to the courthouse to put in an application for a restraining order. Then, I'm going to go to my salon and tell my coworkers that I have left Frank. Then I'm going to call the realtor's office and ask if any apartments have opened up. I'm not sure where I will be sleeping tonight, but I'm not worried about that right now. We have lots of good friends; I'll find somewhere to stay."

"Okay," he said, "I'm going to drive to Chris's house and just hang out there."

"Perfect. I will keep in touch with you. Don't be afraid. We are in God's hands."

We got into our cars and slowly drove down the long gravel driveway. I didn't have time for emotions. I knew that I had to leave, and I was glad Charlie and I got out without any confrontations. We left a lot of our belongings behind, but at that moment it didn't matter. All that mattered to me was that we were both safe and that I was doing what I felt I had to do. The steps were out of order from my original plan. Cindy Sprague had advised me to "get an apartment, get a restraining order, and get out." She also told me that "God would open up a window of opportunity for me." I felt that this was that window of opportunity, so I stepped out in faith. I had no idea how anything would work out, but it didn't really matter to me. God was either with me or He wasn't. I knew that He was, and I decided to trust Him completely and just move forward.

I drove straight to the courthouse. Cindy had told me I would have to turn in an application for a restraining order in the morning and then be back by 1:00 to go to court. I just went through the motions. I was directed to a window where I received an application. I just looked at it, and the attendant told me there was a "victim's advocate" office upstairs where I could get some help filling out the application. I was very grateful for any help I could get. I kept the form simple, stating I did not feel safe with my husband because he had frequent outbursts of rage and anger and he often said he "wanted to kill someone." I turned in the application and drove to the salon.

It felt strange pulling up to my place of work with all of my belongings still packed in my car. It was 10 a.m. and the salon had just opened. The only person there was Alessia. I asked her to come into the back room with me, and I said, "I just left Frank. Charlie and I packed up our cars and drove away."

She looked shocked and said, "Oh my gosh! What happened?"

"Well, Frank has always had anger issues, but I found out he has been cheating on me and I think he is also using drugs. I don't feel safe with him, and I have been counseled to get out and put a restraining order on him, so that's what I'm going to do. My hope is that he will get help and maybe we can be reconciled. But for now, this is what I feel I have to do."

She hugged me and said, "Well, I support you. I've had a similar experience in my own past. I had to leave my husband because he was an alcoholic." Then she asked, "Is there anything I can do to help you? Where are you going to go?"

"You can help me by sending out a group text to my coworkers. Keep it simple. Let them know I had to leave Frank, that this is very hard for me, and I want to keep it private. I can't emotionally afford any drama right now." I told her I was on my way to find out if an apartment opened up for me and I was also going to go to court at 1:00 to try to get a restraining order put on Frank. "I will keep in touch with you. I will either need some help getting a bed into an apartment or sleeping on your sofa."

She hugged me again and said, "Anything you need. Just let me know."

I thanked her and walked out to my car. I got inside and locked the door. I sat there for a minute thinking, *This is crazy.* Then I thought, *Just go moment by moment. The next step is to go down to the realtor's office to find out about an apartment.* My cell phone rang. It was the realtor's office. I said, "This is Rose."

It was Judy. "I have some good news! A one-bedroom apartment opened up today over on Walnut Grove Avenue. It has on-site security, and it's $1,000 a month. The property manager's name is Paul. He said he could show you the apartment today, if you'd like, and that you can move in right away."

"Hold on a second . . . this is great news!" I fumbled for my notebook and a pen. I said, "You won't believe this, but I just left my husband this morning. All my belongings are in my car."

"Oh, I'm so glad that you're safe. You will love this apartment complex."

Then she gave me the address and Paul's phone number. I thanked her for her help. It was amazing. But still, I just sat there in my car. "Breathe," I said to myself. "You don't have time for fear. God is with you. Just keep moving forward."

I felt sick. I didn't feel hungry, but I was having a hard time breathing and my stomach started to hurt. I thought about how God was guiding me, and I knew that I could trust Him. I felt fear wanting to overtake me. I sat there in my car trying to breathe. I thought about the day I got baptized. I remembered going all the way under the water and letting go of everything. I remembered how calm I felt when I got out of the water. I remembered the absence of fear, and I was not about to let it come back. I quietly thanked God for what He was doing even though I didn't like it. I thanked Him and told Him that I trusted Him.

I started the engine and pulled out of the salon parking lot. The apartment wasn't far; that would be nice. I came to a stoplight and looked up through the windshield at the sky. It was such a beautiful day! The sky was deep blue with just a few lazy clouds here and there. I thought, *How weird, while my world is falling apart, someone is out there having a good day.* The stoplight seemed to take forever to turn green. I looked out the window again at the beautiful day. It didn't seem fair. "Right now, at this very moment, someone is at Disneyland standing in line to go on the Matterhorn ride!" The light turned green, and as I drove toward the apartment, I told myself, "When this all settles down, I'm going to plan a trip to California! I want to go to Disneyland! I trust that God is going to bring me through this hard time, and I will be happy again."

11

CHAPTER

The Apartment

When I arrived at the Walnut Grove apartment complex, I was excited that it was so close to work. It was a small complex, surrounded by large beautiful trees with grassy areas between each building. It felt like a hiding place. In fact, it wasn't easy to find. I passed the street on my way there because it wasn't off a main intersection.

I knocked on the property manager's door. As I waited, I glanced at my phone. It was 11:30. I had to be back at the courthouse by 1:00. Everything was falling into place perfectly. The property manager's name was Paul. He was very kind, and he told me he would show me the empty apartment to see if it would work for me. As I followed him across the property, I noticed a small swimming pool. I love to swim and summer was on its way. I was thinking, "Wow, God is opening all of this up for me."

The one-bedroom apartment was an upstairs unit. It was perfect. I knew I would feel safe upstairs. As Paul showed me around the unit, I found it hard to concentrate. I noticed a row of beautiful trees just outside the bedroom window. There were buds on the branches. Winter was finally over and we were experiencing a beautiful spring. The bedroom was large with a walk-in closet. The rest of the apartment had a very open feel. From the kitchen, you could look out over the sink into the dining and living rooms. And past the rooms was a large sliding glass door that led to a balcony. There were lots of windows, and the view was of the west. I started to imagine how lovely the evening sun would look, coming into the rooms.

Paul was explaining something to me about the electrical outlets and how often the filter needed to be changed. I was trying to be casual, but all I could think about was getting back to the courthouse by 1:00. I thanked him and told him that the apartment was perfect. He gave me the key and his phone number. He welcomed me to the complex and told me to call him if I had any questions.

I walked down the stairs toward my car. The sun was still shining, the air was cool and clean, and I had a key to an apartment in my hand. It was all happening fast, and I wasn't afraid. I felt like God was orchestrating the whole day, like I was in the middle of a miracle. I sat in my car and sent Charlie a text: "We have an apartment! I'm on my way to court, so I'll call you when I'm done there."

When I got to the courthouse, the victim's advocate was

there. She asked me if I would like for her to sit with me in court. I said, "Yes, please. I've never done anything like this before, and it's not easy. I could use your support."

She told me that my case for putting a restraining on my husband wasn't very strong. "You haven't been physically hurt, and it's very possible that the judge won't give you the order."

"I'm not worried about it. I'm just doing what I feel I have to do. If he doesn't give me the order, I guess I don't need it."

About halfway through the proceeding, I was starting to find it difficult to breathe. There were a lot of people in the room, and the judge was dealing with one applicant at a time. The fact that I was about to ask a judge to put a restraining order on my husband was weighing heavily on me. The victim's advocate put her arm around my shoulder. I took a deep breath and relaxed. "I'm just going moment by moment here, Lord; you're in control. Thank you for having this advocate here for me."

The judge called my name. "Edith Rose Carver, please stand." I stood up. He spent a few minutes flipping through my application. Then he looked up at me and asked if Frank had ever hit me.

"No."

He flipped through the pages again. Then he said, "It says here that Frank sometimes gets angry and that he has punched a fence near your face."

"Yes."

"And you want me to put a restraining order on him because he has anger outbursts and has said, 'I'm gonna kill someone'?"

I opened my mouth and confidently said, "Yes, your honor, I just don't want that someone to be me."

The judge looked at me and then flipped through the pages again. After a couple minutes he said, "Okay, I'm just going to give it to you. The sheriff will inform you about the details of the restraining order in the lobby. You may be excused."

I walked out into the lobby with the victim's advocate, and she introduced me to the sheriff. I hugged her and thanked her for all her help. The sheriff explained to me the details of how a restraining order works. He told me, "This afternoon, an officer will drive to Frank's house and serve the order to him." The restraining order was good for one year and during that year, Frank was not allowed to be near me. He explained that if I could see Frank walking toward me from across the street, he was too close and I could call 911 and have him arrested. He said, "He can call or text you only because you requested that stipulation." I had included that in the application, hoping we would be able to talk and possibly reconcile. I thanked the officer for explaining everything to me and walked out of the courthouse.

Walking across the parking lot towards my car, I thought about being scared but quickly pushed the fear from my mind. I thought about my baptism day and how all fear had left me. I got into my car and sat there in the parking lot. My car was still filled with all of the items I had taken out of my room that morning. "What a crazy day! What do I do now?" I realized that I hadn't eaten. I paused and whispered a prayer. "Thank you, Lord, for being with me and giving me courage. This has been a strange and hard day, and it's not even over with yet. Thank you for protecting Charlie and me. Thank you for all the people who have helped me today. Please go before me and help me as I go step by step. I've never experienced anything like this, and I'm trying to be brave. I know that you are with me and that you love me. And I know that you are good. I trust you."

After my prayer, I wiped the tears from my face and called Charlie. I told him that the judge gave me a restraining order and that Frank was not allowed to come near me.

He asked, "What are you going to do now?"

"I'm going to go get something to eat, and then I'm going to ask Alessia if she would help me bring a few things from storage into the new apartment."

"Do you mind if I stay with Chris' family tonight?" Charlie asked.

"Of course not. It's been a big day. God is with us. I'm going to set the apartment up with a few basics and go to bed. Then I'm going to go to work in the morning."

"Okay mom," he said. "I can't believe this is happening. I love you."

I forced myself to eat some lunch. It was so hard to chew and to swallow. I felt so sad. I couldn't stop crying. I felt like my heart was breaking. After eating what I could, I called my mom and told her about the events of the day. She asked me if I wanted her to get on a plane and come help me. I told her, "No, not yet. I'm not afraid. I feel like God is with me and He is giving me courage. I'm just going through one thing at a time. Moment by moment." I told her I was going to have a friend help me get a few things into the apartment and that I was planning to work the next day. She assured me that she loved me and that she would be praying for me. I asked her to let my family know for me. I was too tired and had too much to do to. She said that she would.

After that I drove to the new apartment. I parked in my new parking spot and walked up to the apartment. It was completely empty. I walked through each room. It was clean and comfortable. I felt safe. I went downstairs to my car and brought up all of the things I had taken out of my room early in the day. Was that just this morning? After I brought up everything from my car, I looked around and realized I didn't have a bed to sleep on or a pillow. I called Alessia and asked her if she wouldn't mind helping me with a few things.

"Yes. Let me know what you need and I'll bring it to you," she said.

I asked her if I could borrow a pillow and a glass for water and a coffee cup. "Oh," I said, "and maybe a pot so I can boil some water for instant coffee in the morning."

She said she would come over in the evening as soon as she got off work.

It was 4:30 in the afternoon. I got a text on my phone from Frank:

"Hey Rose, I just got served a restraining order from the cops. Could you call me and explain please?"

I looked at the text, and I didn't want to respond. I didn't want to talk with him. I wasn't sure what to do so I didn't do anything. I got another text:

"So I take it you're leaving me? I wish you would talk to me. But if you and Charlie need to get the rest of your stuff, I won't be around to bother you. I love you."

I still didn't know what to say so I didn't say anything. All I knew was that I was running out of daylight and I needed to prepare for the night. I had to work in the morning. I decided to drive to the storage unit. I knew I had a twin mattress there and enough items to eventually fill the apartment. So I drove down and loaded the mattress into my car. I was grateful I had an SUV. I was grateful I had the key to the storage unit on my keychain. Frank had lost his key, and I was meaning to replace it, but I never did. I decided to just gather a few things and then every day after work in the coming weeks, I would drive to the storage unit and bring a carload back to the apartment. I wasn't in a hurry. I was just happy to be safe.

When I got back to the apartment, I received another text from Frank:

> *"I didn't say anything to mom so that it's not uncomfortable for you. But if you would please call me. My heart is breaking right now."*

Then more texts:

> *"I'm so sorry, Rose!"*

> *"My lovely just told me yesterday you would never leave me. I can't understand why you are upset. We were in love."*

Alessia arrived, so I asked her to help me bring the twin mattress up the stairs. I could respond to his texts later. What was I going to say anyway? He would deny all of my accusations. Alessia helped me bring up the mattress, and she also brought two boxes full of supplies. It was very sweet. There were some drinking glasses and coffee cups, a few utensils, some instant coffee, and the saucepan I had requested. She also brought a pillow.

"Oh, do you have sheets and blankets?" she asked.

"Well, I have everything I need in our storage unit. I just forgot to grab some sheets and a blanket."

"You are welcome to stay the night with us."

I told her I appreciated the offer, but I was so tired I could just sleep on the bare mattress.

"I have a small blanket in my car," she said. "You can use it for as long as you need it."

I thanked her and walked down the stairs with her to her car. She pulled out a blanket from her trunk. It was a lap blanket with the Raiders football logo on it. I looked at her haltingly. She smiled and I said, "Oh no! Is that the only blanket you have? I'm not sure I could sleep under a Raiders blanket! I hate the Raiders!" We both laughed and hugged each other. I thanked her for everything and told her I would see her at work in the morning.

When I got back inside the apartment, I sat down on the mattress and sent Frank a text:

> *"I will always love you. Nothing can change that. You've known for a long time that things were bad and that if you weren't going to change your behavior that this would happen. I'm afraid of you. I need you to stay away from me and let me heal."*

Frank responded:

> *"I didn't know this was gonna happen. But I'll leave you alone. I love you so much, Rose. I'll do anything to get you and Charlie back. Please work with me. And if you need anything, let me know."*

"One more thing Rose, I'll go to counseling tomorrow and won't stop until I'm fixed. Please don't give up on me. Just let me know what you want from me. I won't bother you again until you call me. I love you."

I sent Frank a response:

"I know that you are broken and a mess. I know that because I was once rescued out of my miserable state by God Himself. I believe that God is able to help you but it's up to you. It's not a quick or easy journey but you can start by humbly confessing to Him and asking Him to help. I can't help you. You're in God's hands. But you can know that Charlie's and my hearts are broken. We love you. Please stay away and give us space."

There was no response from Frank that night.

I set up my toothbrush and my toiletries in the bathroom. I put the few utensils in one of the empty drawers in the kitchen and put the saucepan on the stove for the morning's coffee. I sent Charlie a text letting him know I was safe in the apartment and going to bed. Then I went into the empty bedroom and looked at the mattress and pillow nudged up against the corner of the room. There were no sheets or pillow cases, just Alessia's horrible Raiders blanket. It looked welcoming. I was exhausted. I turned off the light and lay down on the mattress. I had forgotten to close the window blind, so a soft light from outside was shining into the room. I looked at the ceiling. The mattress and pillow were a welcome support to my tired body. I pulled up the Raiders blanket, and it was surprisingly comfortable. I had no idea what lay ahead of me, but I felt safe. Not just because I was away from a man I had learned not to trust. I felt safe because I was learning to trust someone I could not see. There was a sense of peace around me. I slept well that night, perfectly comfortable as if I were a child, safe in her Father's home.

12

CHAPTER

You Are Brave

Three weeks passed by without a word from Frank. I wasn't sure why he was not contacting me. Maybe he was being passive-aggressive? Maybe he turned himself into a rehab center? I had no idea, and I felt my last text said enough. I felt no need to contact him. Yet I was curious. What was he doing? Was he spending time with his girlfriend? Was he doing drugs?

I fell into a new routine. Every morning I would wake up with the sun. I still hadn't closed the blinds in my bedroom window. I enjoyed looking out at the trees across the yard. They were starting to get new flowers. I felt safe in my upstairs unit. I would make myself a cup of coffee and open up my Bible to read a few passages. I looked forward to spending time in God's Word. It felt like His presence was right there with me, comforting and encouraging me.

Then I would get ready for work and head out the door. I always locked the doors of the car as soon as I got in. I guess I was trying to keep the fear outside. There was nothing to be afraid of. God had opened all these doors for me. It was obvious to me that He was with me and would protect me from any danger. Still, I locked myself into my car and into my apartment.

I did my best to get through each workday. My clients noticed I was quickly losing weight. It was so hard for me to eat and even harder to digest my food properly. My situation made me feel sick. I was trying to be brave, but my heart was breaking. Without going into detail, I let my clients know I had separated from my husband and was going through a difficult time. I told them I may not be as talkative as usual because I needed to concentrate on my work. I told myself that if my personal life kept me from doing my best work, I would have to stop working and probably go back to Greenville and live with my mom for a while. But thankfully, I was able to put my personal situation behind me while at work, and my clients were very supportive.

After work, I drove to our storage unit to gather some boxes and whatever furniture I could fit into my car. I felt scared. I opened the door to the unit and looked at all of our household belongings. It brought back so many memories. I just stood there, looking into the unit, with tears streaming down my face. I was also afraid that Frank would show up and be angry with me for leaving him. I kept my phone in my back pocket. I guess if he showed up, I would call 911.

Or maybe I would just get back into my car and lock the door and call 911. I had to put all my fears and emotions behind me to focus on the task at hand. It would take weeks to unload the storage unit, so I decided I would just come every few days after work and bring a carload of items back to the apartment. My plan was to empty the storage unit completely so I would no longer have to make a monthly payment for it.

My sister had given me some great advice. She said, "I know it's going to be hard for you to unload your storage unit. I want you to take your time doing it. When you open a box, look at each item and ask yourself if it's something that you need to keep and if it still brings you joy. Then, get rid of everything that no longer serves you."

I was grateful to have something to do while I waited to find out if Frank wanted to reconcile with me. I took my time bringing all of the items from my car, up the stairs, and into the apartment. The evening sun was shining into the living room, now getting filled up with my items from storage. I decided to open the boxes marked "kitchen" first so I could start getting settled in. I sat on the floor next to a box. I guess it didn't matter which one I opened first. I said a prayer, "Dear Lord, thank you for being with me. I don't like this part of the journey I'm on, but I know that you are with me. Give me the courage to keep moving forward. Be with me as I go through so many memories. My heart is breaking, Lord; please be with me."

I opened the first kitchen box, and it was full of items

wrapped in tissue. *Probably glasses*, I thought. *Good*! I was excited to set up my new kitchen. I grabbed the first glass and unwrapped the tissue. It was the beautiful amber-colored blown-glass goblet we used for our first communion together at our wedding! I sat back and looked at the glass. *You've got to be kidding me*! I could feel tears wanting to come to my eyes. I looked at the glass and asked myself, "Does this item still bring me joy?" The answer was no. Then I asked, "Will this glass still serve me?" The answer was, "I don't know." I stood up and placed the glass on top of the refrigerator. "I guess it can stay there for now." I didn't cry. I didn't have time to. There were many boxes to unpack, and I was eager to get my new home set up and comfortable. I spent the rest of the evening unpacking. It started to get fun. By bedtime, my kitchen felt comfortable. I turned on the soft light over the stove and looked at the countertops. I now had a wood dish drying rack on the counter and a blue dish towel hanging off one of the door handles. There was a small blue bucket filled with spoons and large utensils now sitting next to my cobalt blue Kitchen Aid mixer. There was a red tea pot sitting on the stove, ready to boil water for my coffee in the morning. It was starting to feel like home.

I went into my bedroom to get ready for bed. The room was also starting to come together. Charlie and his friends had helped me get my queen bed up the stairs, and I was able to set it up with my favorite sheets and comforter. I sat down on the edge of the bed and looked at my phone to set my alarm for morning. Still no text from Frank.

I checked my email account, and there was a message from a realtor. *Who is this and why are they sending me an email?* I opened the message and it was addressed to me— from a woman I had never met. She was asking if I was still interested in purchasing a house and listed the address. I figured it must have been a mistake. Maybe someone was returning an earlier request from me when I was desperate to find a place to live. I was about to delete the email when I paused. Beneath her signature, address, and phone number was a link to a song. The title of the song was "You Make Me Brave." *That's weird*, I thought, then decided to listen to the song.

I plugged my earphones into my phone, turned off the light, and lay down on my bed. The window blind was still wide open, which allowed a few gentle shadows from the streetlight to fill my room. I clicked on the link for the song and was immediately overwhelmed. As I listened to the music and the words of the song, I imagined myself standing at the edge of a deep, dark ocean. I could feel my feet in the water and could almost smell the salty air. I love the ocean and know how to swim past the waves but in my imagination, the waves were too strong and the waters too dark, stretching out to an unknown horizon. I laid there crying, listening to the song over and over again. As I drifted off to sleep, I thought to myself, *I am brave. The Lord has called me to follow Him to a place I've never been before, and I can trust His love. I think He might be proud of me.*

The next morning, I called the realtor from the email. She answered and I said, "Hello, my name is Rose Carver. I received an email from you regarding a house for sale and I wanted to let you know that I am not looking for a house to buy." She said, "Oh, I'm sorry. I'm not sure how your email address was included but I sent that message out to people who had been inquiring about the property." I said, "Oh, that's no problem. I just have a question about the song that you included in the bottom of your email. Why do you have a link to that song there?" She said, "Well, I'm a Christian and that song means a lot to me. I include it on the bottom of all of my emails, hoping it will be a blessing to someone." I told her, "Well, I am going through a very difficult time in my life right now. I know that God is with me and the song you sent blessed me and gave me extra courage to face whatever is next." She said, "Oh wow! This is so awesome! I guess it wasn't sent to you by mistake but by God's plan." I thanked her and said goodbye, knowing that I would probably never meet her in person. I got ready for work with a smile on my face and courage in my heart. I would just go through the day, moment by moment. God was with me; I didn't need to be afraid. I was looking forward to bedtime when I would l snuggle into my cozy bed and listen to the beautiful song again.

13

The Stalking

I spent the next few weeks allowing myself to fall into a new normal. I would wake each morning with the sun shining right into my face from the open window of my bedroom. I would lay on my bed and think about my dreams. I was sleeping soundly and comfortably. It felt like God was visiting me in my dreams. Some of the dreams I would remember, but most I would forget. I marveled at how peaceful I felt through each night.

I would get up out of bed and walk to my bedroom window. I could see the row of trees across the lawn. They were budding and each day I noticed more flowers were starting to appear, as it was spring. Then I would walk to the kitchen and turn on the teakettle for a morning cup of coffee. I started to drink my coffee black. Instant coffee was good enough for me. I couldn't get through a half-gallon of milk on my own before it would go bad. I didn't bother with making breakfast either. Eating food was still a chore for me. Charlie suggested that I buy a protein powder so I could at least drink my breakfast, so some days I would mix the powder with water and drink it down to at least get some nutrition. Then I would sit down with my cup of coffee and open up my Bible. I enjoyed reading anything in the Bible. The words comforted me, and I felt like God Himself was sitting right next to me. Sometimes I would read stories of how others handled difficult situations in their lives. They would trust in God's goodness and He never failed any of them. This gave me the courage to go on.

> *They would trust in God's goodness and He never failed any of them. This gave me the courage to go on.*

Then I would go to work. My coworkers didn't ask many questions, and I appreciated that. While I was at work, I needed to focus on my craft. I would take each workday moment by moment, trusting that God would give me the ability to keep my thoughts and emotions behind me while I was working. One day, Frank called the salon. Gabby answered the phone, and Frank announced himself by his last name of Carver and asked to speak with Tammy.

Gabby interrupted me as I was working and said, "I think Frank is on the phone. He announced himself as Carver and asked to speak with Tammy!" She seemed frightened.

I didn't have time to respond when Tammy walked over to me. She also looked scared. She covered the phone with her hand and said, "I have Frank on hold, and he's asking if he can come in to get a haircut from me. What should I do?"

I said, "You can tell Frank that he cannot come to this salon to get his haircut, or he will go to jail." I was not afraid. On my next break, I sent Frank a text:

> *"Honey, you know that you cannot come to the salon. I don't want to get you into any more trouble than you are already in. If you need to text me, you can. I will text back when I can."*

There was no response. In fact, I didn't hear from Frank for the next three weeks. But I knew what he was up to. My "new normal" included spending hours after work franticly searching through social media, background checks, and any other form of technology I could think of to somehow see what he was doing. Even though I had walked away from Frank and put a restraining order on him, I still longed to know what he was doing. I was separated from my husband, and he was doing nothing to reconcile. I guess I was hoping that Frank would see the error of his ways, turn away from drugs, leave the girlfriend, and run to the nearest church to repent. Being cheated on was a new experience for me, and I really didn't know if our marriage could be saved. I was waiting on Frank's next move, but he was not contacting me at all so I started to stalk him, using technology.

I had access to our joint bank account and to our phone accounts because I was the one who paid the bills in our home. I took advantage of this and could track everything Frank spent money on. In a way, I could follow him through his day. I found that I could also track every phone call and text he sent in real time. This was how I found out that during our last conversation together, Frank was texting his girlfriend while texting me!

I found out that I had access to our cell phone records, going back years. Every night after work, I would stop by our storage unit, load up my car, and head back to the apartment. I would make something to eat, unload a few boxes, and set up some furniture. I had a new system that was working well for me. The apartment was coming together, and I was just going moment by moment with God by my side. But once the responsibilities were done for the night, instead of opening my scriptures to read before bed, I started falling into the habit of getting online to see what Frank had been up to. I spent hours researching his past and present phone activity. It was almost becoming an addiction, and it didn't feel good. In fact, it was making me feel sick and afraid. I didn't like seeing how often he was in contact with his girlfriend. I didn't like looking up so many past phone numbers, only to find them linked to people who had been put in jail for meth use and delivery. I could see when he sent videos or pics to his girlfriend, but I could not see the content. My mind did not imagine that he was sending her sunset pics or videos of himself fishing.

One day, as I was checking into Frank's girlfriend's social media account, I saw that the two of them were in Hawaii! I couldn't believe what I was seeing. There was Frank, with his girlfriend, her son, and her mother, enjoying the sunny sky and warm waters of Hawaii. Hawaii of all places? That is where we spent our honeymoon! It was almost too much to take in. Did Frank place no value on our wedding vows? Did he not understand that we were still married?

After this I sat down and said to myself, "This is disgusting. It is doing you absolutely no good to be wasting all these hours stalking Frank. It's toxic. It's dark and ugly, and it's making you feel sick. It's robbing you of your joy and allowing fear and anger into your heart. You've spent these weeks carefully going through each item you unpack from storage. You've taken the time to let go of what no longer serves you or brings you joy. You've got to stop stalking Frank. You've got to let go completely and trust God. God sees what Frank is doing. He sees Frank's heart. It's time to let Frank be God's problem and not yours. It's time to let go."

So I stopped all the research. I went to the bank and explained to them that I was separated from my husband and wanted to take myself off of the joint account. I had a separate business account that all of my income went into, and that would become my only bank account. I called our phone company and explained my situation. They were able to separate our account by having Frank and I on a conference call. I sent Frank a text, letting him know I wanted to separate our cell phone account and he would have to answer his phone to give the company his permission to do it. He cooperated, and our account was separated. I knew I could not stop stalking Frank's daily and nightly activity with my own willpower, so I cut myself off from being able to look into his business. It felt strange but good. When people would ask me how Frank was doing or what he was up to, I would say, "I have no idea. He's totally in God's hands."

After this, mornings and evenings were again peaceful for me. I decided I would just "stay the course" and trust God with my future. I finished the task of clearing out the storage unit and setting up my new home. I actually had fun going through each item. If it was no longer useful or didn't bring me joy or caused me to feel sad, I let it go. I brought a lot of my kitchen items to a local safe house for youth whose parents were addicts or in jail. It felt great to bless them and to let go of past memories.

One evening when I came home from work, there was a package at my doorstep. It was from my stepmother Abby. I brought the box into the apartment and set it on the dining room table. The apartment was clean and comfortable. The setting sun was pouring soft gold rays of sunshine into the house through the west windows. I went to the kitchen and opened the junk drawer. I grabbed the scissors and opened the package. Inside the box was a beautiful card, a pair of pajamas, a framed picture of a geometric design I knew she had colored herself with colored pencils, and a handmade flannel pillowcase with a geometric design in red, orange, white, and light green.

Tears welled up in my eyes as I opened the package. I was so grateful for my family. Although they lived miles away, they were showing me their love by respecting my wishes to stay in Madison. I spoke on the phone daily with one family member or another and knew in my heart they were all holding me up in prayer. I felt completely loved, and that was important as I was entering into a real season of grief. My marriage was dying or had died, and my heart had been broken.

I had no choice but to allow myself to walk through grief. What this meant to me at the time was to allow myself to cry whenever I felt the tears come. It was usually in the evening when I got home from work, after I had forced myself to eat some dinner and was getting ready to wind down for the night. I would walk out onto the patio and watch the sunset. I was all alone. I would look at the beautiful sky or watch a bird flutter around in a tree, and the tears would come. I wouldn't stop them. It seemed healthy to let myself cry when it was time to cry. I had faith that God would bring me through this new season of grief and that I wouldn't cry forever. I believed that God could heal a broken heart.

CHAPTER

The Journal

There was one last little gift in the package that I received from my stepmother Abby—a beautiful teal-colored leather-bound journal. There was a pattern embossed on the cover, and it felt good to the touch. There were also gold words imprinted on the front cover that said, "For He shall give His angels charge over you. To keep you in all your ways" (Psalm 91:11).

I opened the journal to look inside. On the top of each page was a beautifully printed Bible verse. Under the verse was a blank lined page. A journal. It had been years since I had kept a journal. In my teens I had a diary, which I filled up. In my twenties I kept several journals. I used to spend time filling up my journals with thoughts, dreams, poems, and questions about life. But it had been years. As I held this beautiful journal in my hands, I knew it was time again to write.

I was still attending Cindy Sprague's Tuesday night classes on domestic abuse. One evening after class, Cindy took me aside and asked if I would consider writing a book about my experience. "Rose, I am so excited and amazed at what God has done for you. Others need to hear this. Would you consider writing a book about your experience? Even if you just kept a journal of what you are going through, it would be so encouraging for others who need to take the steps you took. You are an example of what God can do."

I looked at her and said, "I will. I believe that the Lord wants me to share my experience. Right now, I'm still in the middle of it, but I've been given a journal. I will commit to writing in this journal for one year. After that, I will write and publish a book about it. I believe that the Lord hears the cries of the innocent. If what I am going through gives just one person the courage to believe in God's love and trust Him, it will be worth it."

That night after class, I went into my bedroom and turned on the lamp that hung over my small antique school desk. The lampshade was made of pressed paper, and it gave a soft glow. My beautiful new journal was lying on top of the desk. I sat down in the chair and opened up the journal. I looked at the blank lines on the first page and read the Bible scripture that was at the heading: "For I know the plans I have for you, declares the Lord, plans to prosper you

and not to harm you, plans to give you hope and a future"
(Jeremiah 29:11).

I sat back on the chair and started to cry. This was the
same verse my godmother had written in a card she sent to
me just a few months before her death. This was the same
verse that was painted in watercolor and framed and given to
Frank and I as a wedding gift. I was no stranger to this verse.
I had read it many times and had hoped that it would be
true for my life. But here I sat, alone in my new apartment,
separated from my husband, trying my best to trust God
moment by moment.

I stood up, blew my nose and washed my face. I was
determined to start this journal. I picked up a pencil and
wrote down the first entry:

JOURNAL ENTRY: 4/11/16

*Charlie and I left Circle Drive at 8:00 a.m.
after Frank left for work and while Patricia was
asleep. We left Lady, Daisy, Max, and Casper.
We left some furniture and a few items. I drove
to the Courthouse and submitted a restraining
order on Frank. I drove to the realtor's office and
signed a lease for the Walnut Grove apartment.
I went to the apartment and got the keys. I
went to court at 1:00 pm and got the restraining
order. At 4:30 p.m., Frank was served.*

I closed the journal and thought to myself, *This is going*

to be hard but I'm going to do it. I felt sad as I sat there. I decided to open up my Bible. I wanted to read something that would comfort me. I opened up my Bible to Psalm 23, hoping reading it would make me feel better. I read it and I didn't feel better because of the part that says, "Yea though I walk through the valley of the shadow of death, I will fear no evil." I stood up and paced the bedroom. How do I handle this? What do I do with this psalm? I don't think I like it anymore.

Then the tune of my mother's lullaby came to my mind. It was the twenty-third psalm, and it was my favorite as a child. I knew the tune and each word by heart. I used to sing it to Charlie when he was small. I started to hum the song. I wanted it to comfort me like it did when I was a child, but I was afraid to sing it because of the "valley of the shadow of death" verse. I gathered my courage and sat down at my small desk again. I opened the journal and picked up the pencil. I would sing the song and write down the words as I sang. I hated what I was going through. I did not like the fact that my loving Heavenly Father was allowing me to go through such a difficult time. I did not want to see my Good Shepherd as one who would guide me into grief. But there I was, so I sat down and sang. Tears dropped onto the page of my new journal as I sang and wrote the words:

> *The Lord is my Shepherd*
> *I shall not want*
> *He maketh me to lie down*

In green pastures
He leadeth me beside the still waters
He restoreth my soul
He leadeth me
In the paths of righteousness
For His name's sake
Yea though I walk through the valley
Of the shadow of death
I will fear no evil
For Thou art with me
Thy rod and Thy staff they comfort me
Thou preparest a table before me
In the presence of mine enemies
Thou anointeth my head with oil
My cup runneth over
Surely goodness and mercy
Shall follow me
All the days of my life
And I shall dwell
In the House of The Lord
Forever

—Psalm 23

When I got to the verse about the "valley of the shadow of death," I stopped singing for a moment. I dropped my face into my hands and sobbed aloud. My body shook with grief, not just because my husband was cheating on me but because my Good Shepherd had led me into this dark valley. In my mind, I saw innocent sheep being led through a very scary and dangerous valley. Why would the Good Shepherd lead his sheep into such a valley? It's too hard. It's just heartbreaking. I sat there crying, with the pencil still in my hand, staring at the words I had just written in the journal: "Yea though I walk through the valley of the shadow of death." I took a deep breath and thought to myself, *You know what? I trust this Shepherd. If He wants to lead me into a scary valley, I will follow.* I wiped the tears from my face and continued writing as I sang the rest of the song. It felt good to get through the whole song. I was glad I did not allow myself to avoid reading that psalm. I was not going to allow my circumstances to make this scripture ugly. I love that psalm, and I will sing it even if it breaks my heart. Because I trust the Good Shepherd.

15

CHAPTER

Stay The Course

They say that "time heals all wounds." I don't agree with that, but I do agree with the saying, "Time passes," especially when you are waiting for a miracle. I had disciplined myself to be totally cut off from my husband. I was leaving the ball in his court, so to speak. I had nothing to say to him that I hadn't already said, and I was no longer stalking him through social media or cell phone activity. I was hoping Frank would text me and ask for a phone conversation. I was praying he would run to the altar and give his life to Jesus and ask me to forgive him. I knew I made the right decision when I walked out of Frank's life that day, and I was grateful for the restraining order. It gave me a timeline. I had one year to be away from his lies and dangerous behavior. I had one year to keep a journal. I guess I was giving God one year to perform a miracle.

Each day I was getting stronger and healthier. I was learning to trust God completely and was falling into a more disciplined lifestyle. My mother reminded me that I seem to be most comfortable in life when I am surrounded by structure, so I allowed myself to be structured.

> *I was giving God one year to perform a miracle.*

When I woke up each morning, I would make my bed and get a cup of coffee. I would spend time reading the Bible and praying. I would go to work and do the best job I could. In the evenings, I would make dinner and either listen to music or watch a movie. Then I would write in my journal. At the end of each day, I would read another scripture in the Bible and pray. Then I would fall asleep content that God was in control and He cared about me.

I started to fill up any free time in my schedule with other activities. I started to teach myself how to play the guitar, and I joined a tap-dancing class. I didn't want to give myself too much free time. I didn't want to be tempted to start stalking Frank's activities again, and I didn't want to allow myself to become too sad or afraid. I also kept in close contact with my family in Greenville. I was able to spend one weekend a month with a family member, either in Greenville or in Madison.

This was helping the time to go by more easily. I also spent as much time as I could in church. I felt safe and comfortable there. I would go to the Saturday night service and then again to the Sunday morning service. I would also go to the mid-week service. One time the church had a "Family Testimony Night." It was a very casual setting, and the pastor encouraged anyone who wanted to share something to come to the microphone. As different people started to share, I became encouraged. I felt like these words were being spoken just for me. I took a small notepad and pen out of my purse and wrote down some of the things that people said.

"Moment by moment, God is faithful. With God, all things are possible."

"Life is worth getting up for and worth getting dressed for."

"God is my Father. God loves me like a parent."

"Stay the course. God will navigate you through the dark waters."

"I'm here for a reason."

"God is preparing us for these last days. Cling to the Lord."

"Stay the course in the Word and in fellowship."

"Stay the course, buckle into Christ."

"Follow Him with obedience and a joyful heart."

"Obey God because we want to, out of love, not because we have to."

"Allow yourself to be fully in love with Jesus."

"God is in control. Trust Him. Everything is going to be okay. God is in control."

"God had His hold on you. Follow Him."

"Sometimes life gets bumpy before it gets better. God will never leave you."

"Some of the greatest people start out hard. Don't wonder why sometimes God allows sorrows to come into our lives."

"Have faith. Worship. God will sustain us through troubled times."

I was filling up my time with structure, positive thoughts, and fun activities. I was trying to avoid grief, but it came whenever it wanted to. If I felt a wave of grief coming while I was at work, I would push it back. I would say to myself, "I'll cry about this later." And I would. Many times, the tears would start flowing before I could even leave the parking lot. I would have to sit in my car and cry before driving home.

One night when I was writing in my journal, I became very angry. I had heard that sometimes anger is a part of grieving, so I just let myself write down an angry entry.

It's been three months. I'm tired and very, very angry. I don't know what I'm waiting for. My husband is an idiot and he has hurt me horribly. Do I wait for a miracle? And what does a miracle look like? At this point I want to either divorce him or kill him or both. I am pissed. I don't want to give him the satisfaction of a text from me, even an angry one. The silence is stronger.

I put down my pen. This was the first time I wrote down the word "divorce." I was very angry, but I knew I didn't want to kill Frank. I wasn't sure what to do with these feelings. I decided I would go outside and have an angry talk with God.

I walked out the front door and down the stairs to the parking lot. It was dark and the night sky was full of stars. *Oh good*, I thought, *I'll look up to the stars and imagine God looking down at me from behind the stars, and I'll let him know how angry I am.* I looked up and before I opened my mouth, tears started to roll down my cheeks. I shrugged it off. They were tears of anger, and

I had something to say. I opened my mouth and said, "Heavenly Father, I am so, so angry! Do you see . . ." But I couldn't speak another word. I was going to say, "Do you see how angry I am?" but my voice just stopped. I stood there staring at the stars, unable to say another word. And as I stood there, silenced, I could hear God's response in my mind. He said, "Yes, I see. I see a child looking up at me, saved by grace. I see a child forgiven, unearned and undeserved. And I love you."

This was the last time I would ever feel anger toward Frank. I didn't like how it felt. I walked back up the stairs and into my bedroom. I opened up my journal and wrote down another entry.

JOURNAL ENTRY: 7/6/16 - 11:45pm

My Goals:
1) Grieve my lover.
2) Get divorced - leave Frank in God's hands.
3) Enjoy my sweet son for a season.
4) Grow in grace and faith.
5) Become debt free and financially secure.
6) Enjoy Madison, Green Valley Church, my friends, and the salon.
7) October - maybe change job.
8) January - maybe move back to Greenville.
9) Finish Bible college.
10) Get involved in missions trips.

11) Continue swimming, eating healthy, and staying strong.
12) Live fully within God's will. Be used by Him.

Filling my days with goals and structure helped me to "stay the course." I could not see what the future held but God could. And I let myself trust Him. Time can't heal but God can. I was beginning to enjoy writing in the journal. Some days were hard, some days were easy, and some days were fun! I started to realize that maybe God wanted to write my story. As I flipped back through the pages of the journal, I realized I did not need to wait for a miracle. I was in one.

16

Do I Matter?

I was pleasantly surprised by how well I was able to sleep each night. I felt safe and comfortable in my new apartment. I felt that God was with me, protecting me during the day and comforting me during the night. Most nights I would dream. They were usually pleasant dreams and I always woke up thinking, *That was interesting.* But then, I would usually forget the dream by the time I was fully awake. One morning when I woke up, I remembered my dream vividly. I decided to write about it in my journal.

JOURNAL ENTRY: 7/17/16

This morning I remembered the dream I had. I was given a sapphire wedding ring. It was beautiful but when I woke up, I thought it was strange since I have no interest in ever getting married again. Maybe there is a different meaning.

I Googled it:

"Sapphire Wedding Ring - Should not be enhanced, only heated. Symbolism: Sapphire is the gemstone of truth, purity, blessings, and knowledge. Royalty and high priests often used the sapphire in their own rings to symbolize their blessings as divine holders of knowledge and wisdom."

Maybe God made me with the unique ability to be a leader or a teacher? Maybe He wants to use me to guide others to Himself? Maybe I am different. With His help I can see other people as simply His creation whom He loves and not be afraid to be used by Him. May God's will be done.

Even though I was sleeping well and dreaming wonderful dreams in the night, some days were harder to get through than others. Some days seemed so long. I was grateful for my new structure and happy distractions, but there were times when I would be alone and just wonder why I was going through such an emotionally painful experience.

It had been two whole months since I'd received a text

from Frank. Why wasn't he contacting me? I was sure he would have at least tried to save our marriage. The last photograph I saw of him on Facebook, before I cut myself off from looking, was a photo of him standing with his family in front of my sister-in-law's house. His dad and step-mom had finally come to Madison for a visit. I never got to meet them in person. They lived clear across the continent and always talked about flying or driving to Madison to meet Charlie and I, but they never did. Frank had flown to their house two or three times during the eleven years we were married, but Charlie and I were never invited to go along. I didn't question it at the time because flights were expensive. But now I had all the time in the world to realize my rejection. And it didn't feel good.

I wrote another entry into my journal, a prayer to God.

JOURNAL ENTRY: 7/19/16

Who am I that You should care? I am just one soul among many. Do you see my tears? My broken heart? My longings yet unfulfilled? My life is fleeting. Do I matter?

I see You using me to encourage the people that You bring across my path. There is no discrimination. You use me to encourage them all. Any race, any religion, any brokenness. All who are confused, lost, and lonely. Your love reaches out to all of them.

Who am I that Your eyes would land upon me?
I feel rejected. I want to matter.

Rejection is a painful thing to go through. All those years I thought I was the most important person in the world to my husband, I never imagined he would cheat on me. I never imagined that our marriage wouldn't last forever. I trusted his love towards me. Yet this was not the first time I felt rejected by someone I trusted. When my father left my mother for another woman, I also felt rejected. Yet, the very night that my father moved out of our home, my mother sat my sisters, my brother, and me all down and said, "Your father has exchanged the truth for a lie. You need to forgive him so your heart will stay right. God's love is bigger than this situation. He will never leave you. You need to trust God with all your heart and forgive your father."

I was starting to realize that the rejection of my father in my past was serving to give me the courage to handle my present feelings of rejection from my husband. I did what my mother suggested, and I forgave my father. Even though I spent the rest of my childhood without a father in my life, my siblings and I never doubted the love and care of our Heavenly Father. And in my early adulthood, I reconciled with my father and my relationship with him as an adult was better than it was when I was a child. I decided I would not fall apart over rejection. It's real and it's painful, but I knew from experience that God would not reject me.

Before I went to bed that night, I walked out the front door and down the stairs. I wanted to look at the night sky and breathe the warm summer air. As I looked at the stars, I thought about a verse in the Bible that I had memorized as a young adult. It was a strange verse, but I was drawn back to it many times over the years. I had also written this verse in Charlie's baby book because I wanted him to know that, although I would do my very best to be an excellent mom, my love for him could never compare to God's love for him.

The verse was from Isaiah 49:15. I said it out loud:

> *"Can a mother forget the baby at her breast and have no compassion on the child she has borne? Though she may forget, I will not forget you!"*

Do I matter? The peace that I felt in my heart said *yes*. The scriptures in the Bible say *yes*. Even the warm summer breeze whispered, "Yes." I matter.

17

The Package

When I go through something difficult, I try to encourage myself by counting down the hours, minutes, or days until the difficulty passes. In school, I would look at the clock and think, *Just two more hours until I can go back outside to play.* If I was stuck in bed with a flu, I would lie there thinking, *In two weeks, this virus will pass and I won't feel sick anymore.*

After I left my husband, I also started to count. At first it was just moment by moment, trying to get through one day at a time. Then I would look at my calendar and count how many days had passed by since I walked away from my husband, leaving him with the ultimatum that unless he changed his behavior, I could not come back. The days turned into weeks, and the weeks turned into months. In all this time, there was no sign of change in Frank. I was hoping for a miracle. I was hoping that our marriage would be saved.

I had been faithfully writing in my journal every day because I had promised Cindy Sprague I would write a book about my experience. I had witnessed God miraculously open up the way for me to get safely out of an abusive relationship, and I felt God wanted me to document my experience for one full year so others could one day read about it and find courage.

But I was just three months into my one-year commitment, and I didn't know how the story was going to end. I was growing impatient. I felt like I was innocent and my heart was breaking. Things were good when I was able to keep a positive attitude, when I was fully trusting God. But some days were more difficult than others.

One evening, after writing an entry in my journal, I lost my patience. I was writing about how maybe I should just leave the country for a while, do some missions work in Mexico for my church, and just get away, when I suddenly stopped writing and threw my journal into the corner of the room.

What's the point?! I looked over toward the journal, lying face down and open in the corner of the room, and I started to cry. *I don't know what God is doing, and I don't know what He is planning to do, but I hate what I'm going through and I don't want to keep a journal anymore*!

I decided I was not going to write a book. What I was going through was hard enough without writing about it. I decided I would just keep living one day at a time, stay close to the Lord, and wait for my miracle. I left the journal in the corner of the room and went to bed angry.

The next morning went as usual. I woke up, made a cup of coffee, and opened up my Bible to read a scripture. The passage I opened up to was Micah 7:7: "But as for me, I watch in hope for the Lord, I wait for God my Savior; my God will hear me."

This passage comforted me, and as I drove off to work I thought, *I will just keep doing what I'm doing and pray for God to give me the endurance I need to keep moving forward. There is no magic timeline that I can count down to, so I have no choice but to simply trust God.*

When I got home from work that evening, there was a package sitting on the mat in front of my apartment door. I picked it up and brought it into my bedroom. It was from my niece Diana! How fun to receive a package from home! I opened the box and enjoyed slowly unwrapping each gift. There was a lovely scented candle, a beautiful pair of silk pajamas with a cherry blossom print, and a journal. *A journal?!*

Yes, a beautiful leather teal-colored journal almost exactly like the one that was still lying on the floor in the corner of the room. I held the new journal in my hands and looked it over. The cover was made of a textured leather with more embossing than the one Abby had given me, but it was the exact same color.

I knew immediately that God wanted me to continue

keeping a journal. This was no coincidence. I walked over to the corner of the room and picked up the journal from Abby. I glanced at my last entry and closed the pages. I looked at the scripture that was embossed on the front cover in gold print. It was from Psalm 91:11. It read, "For He shall give His angels charge over you, to keep you in all your ways."

I brought the journal back to my bed and sat down and looked at the new journal from Diana. I couldn't believe my eyes! As I sat there holding both journals in my hands, I was blown away by how much the two journals were almost exactly the same!

I looked again at the new journal from Diana. It had a different Bible verse imprinted on the cover. And it was embossed in purple instead of gold. It had a large cross printed on it and under the cross were the words, "With God all things are possible," Matthew 19:26.

I opened up the new journal to see if there were scripture passages printed at the top of each page, like Abby's journal, and there were! I read the scripture that was on the first page. It was Jeremiah 29:11:

> *"For I know the plans I have for you," declares the Lord, "plans to prosper you and not to harm you, plans to give you hope and a future."*

I sat back on my bed and looked out the bedroom window. The blinds were still up and I could see the setting sunlight on the row of trees that were now full of leaves.

Summer was here, and the days were getting longer. I looked down at the two beautiful journals in my hands. I drew in a deep breath and let out a long sigh. Apparently, I needed to write.

My eyes started to burn as I walked towards the small wood desk in the other corner of my room. I gently laid both journals on the top of the desk. *Yes, I will write.* I set my pencil in the groove of that beautiful old-fashioned school desk and committed to continue keeping a journal for a full year. "Who knows what God will do in a year?"

I decided to stop counting down the days. I realized I had no idea what my future held. I was acutely aware of the fact that the only reason I woke up each morning was because God had granted me another day to live and to breathe. I decided to believe that what I had read in Jeremiah 29:11 could be for me personally—that God does know the plans He has for me and that those plans are very good. I could trust Him with my future. And I would write about the process. Maybe someday the journal would become a book, and the book would encourage someone to hang in there through the hard times.

> *"Who knows what God will do in a year?"*

18

Going Public

It's interesting to live in a small town. Everyone seems to be connected to each other either by family members or friends. A few of my clients were friends of Frank and his family but after I left him, they stopped making appointments with me. I didn't mind. I had no idea what they thought of me or what Frank and his family thought of me. And after four months of trying to explain to everyone why I left Frank, I was happy to go to work and just chat with my clients about the latest events. One of my clients, Max, had worked with Frank for several years before opening up his own company. Max had been my client for the past three years, and he had become a friend. He was a Christian and we had gotten to know each other, and I always enjoyed talking about his family and how his new business was going. Max came in for a haircut, and I wasn't even thinking that he might have been in touch with

Frank. As we walked toward my chair, he asked me how I was doing. I told him that I was doing fine, but he kept looking at me funny. I asked him how he was, and he said, "I'm doing okay, but I'm just concerned about how you're doing since Frank went public on Facebook."

"What do you mean?" I asked.

He just sat there looking at me with a strange expression on his face, like he regretted his last statement. "Well, Frank 'friend requested' me on Facebook last night, and I accepted his request. When I opened his page, I saw that his status was *In a Relationship with Sally Martin*."

I looked at Max, shrugged my shoulders, and said, "That's lame." Then I turned his chair toward the mirror, draped the haircutting apron over his shoulders, and prepared myself to give him a haircut. This was not the first time I had to put my emotions behind me to concentrate at work. I'd been through an emotional roller coaster over the last four months, and I had learned how to focus on the task at hand. My emotions would have to wait until after the haircut.

I told Max I had put Frank completely into God's hands and I was just waiting. I told him that I was going day by day and moment by moment, trusting God to guide me into the next step. He told me he was very sorry all this was happening to me and that he and his wife would be praying for me. He also said if I needed anything, to call him. I appreciated the love and support I felt from my clients.

When I got home from work that evening, the sun was shining beautifully into the dining room. The house was comfortable just as I had left it that morning. But there was a darkness that was threatening to come in. I looked around and thought, *I can just turn on a few lights and make some dinner and put on some music.* That would keep the peaceful feeling. Or I could go into my room and open up my computer to see Frank's new status on Facebook. The choice was mine. I knew that if I chose the latter, I would feel sick and maybe sad or angry, and that the cozy feeling of the house would change to a sort of emotional darkness.

I didn't feel hungry, and I remembered that after weeks of silence from Frank, I had received a text from him yesterday. He had asked me to close his Facebook account. At the time I thought it was a strange request, and I texted back that I didn't know how to close the account. His reply was just "Okay, thanks."

I couldn't resist the temptation to open up my computer. I searched Frank's name and found he had opened up a new account. There it was, *Status: In A Relationship with Sally Martin.* It was so strange that I couldn't even get angry. We were still married, and yet there were photos of my husband and his girlfriend together. I realized it was probably his girlfriend who created the new Facebook account. Frank was never good at that sort of stuff. She was probably just excited about her new relationship.

A strange peace came over me. I wasn't angry or sad or scared. I was actually kind of relieved to see their relationship exposed. Until now, it was just my word against his. Also, I didn't feel like I could justify passing condemnation on them when I had a huge log sticking out of my own eye. My past came flooding back into my memory.

Twenty-four years ago, I'd been in Ms. Martin's shoes. I was in a relationship with a married man who was separated from his wife. I remembered exactly how I felt back then. I didn't care that the man I was with was not divorced yet. He was separated, and that was good enough for me. The wife was somewhere far away. I didn't care too much about how she might have felt if she had known about us. I wasn't caring too much about anybody but myself back then, and those choices cost me a lot.

I didn't envy Frank's position or his girlfriend's. I felt pity for them. But I also realized that it was probably time to get divorced. I closed the computer and went back into the kitchen. I turned on a few lights and started cooking. I put on some music and thought about what I would do for the rest of the evening. I would eat some dinner and maybe watch something on TV. Then I would write in my journal and read some scriptures. God was in control, and I knew He loved me. He had forgiven me, and by His grace I could forgive.

After dinner I watched a show on TV for a little while until I realized I wasn't even hearing what was being said. My mind was somewhere else. I got up, turned off the TV, and walked out the front door. I walked down the steps and out across the grass to the parking lot. I just wanted to be outside. I looked up at the stars. I didn't have a prayer to say, and I wasn't thinking of anything in particular. I just stood there looking up at the stars. My gaze turned toward the horizon. I saw a very sparkly cluster of stars. I looked intently at the cluster. What a strange sight! They were twinkling so intensely that they almost looked like colored Christmas tree lights. I had seen this group of stars before but never sparkling like this.

I drew in a deep breath. The night air smelled good. Summer was almost over. Time was passing, and I was glad. *I think I'll go upstairs and look up that cluster of stars. I can't remember what it's called. Then I'll write in my journal and go to bed. I've done enough thinking for today.*

JOURNAL ENTRY: 8/30/16

I don't want to write this down in my journal, but I guess I will because I also don't want to talk with anyone about it. Two days ago, I felt in my heart that it was time to walk towards divorce. Yesterday I left a message with Cindy asking for her help. I don't know how to get divorced, but today I felt a peace about divorcing Frank.

The stars were beautiful tonight. There was one cluster that was so clear and vivid I felt like I was looking into another dimension! I looked it up online and it's called "Pleiades or Orion's Belt." I thanked God for it because it was beautiful.

Today was a difficult day. I'm not out of the storm, but God is with me. Trust Him and ride it out. Be patient.

19

Sunrise

The morning sunrise came streaming into my bedroom like a public announcement. *Why don't I ever close my blinds?!* I got out of bed and walked to the window. The morning sunshine was delightful. I went to the kitchen and turned on the kettle. I was glad for my new routine. I would have a cup of hot coffee, read a passage in my Bible, and get ready for work. Having a structured daily routine helped me to move forward. I could not afford to spiral down into a deep pit of despair.

I made my cup of coffee and snuggled back into bed to spend a few minutes reading the Bible before getting ready for work. It didn't matter to me which portion of the scriptures I read. When I spend time reading the Bible, I reflect on what God has done for us. When I read about the great things God did back then, I feel encouraged. The theme that runs through all of the scriptures is that God loves us. Sometimes when I read a passage, it feels like God is speaking directly to me!

I sat up on my bed and propped my pillow behind my back. I felt comfortable with the sunshine filling my room and my hot cup of coffee next to me on the nightstand. I only had a few minutes to read before getting ready for work, so I just opened it and started to read. The passage I opened to was Amos 5:8. It said, "He who made Pleiades and Orion, who turns midnight into dawn and darkens day into night, who calls for the waters of the sea and pours them out over the face of the land—the LORD is his name."

I sat back against my pillow. I could not believe what I was reading! Pleiades and Orion?! Wasn't I just staring at those stars last night? Didn't I Google the cluster to find out its name?! I got up from my bed and walked over to my little desk. I had to open my journal to read last night's entry. There it was. I had indeed written down the names of those very stars.

Sometimes we take for granted that the sun will rise in the morning. Maybe that's why I hadn't shut my bedroom blinds for almost five months. If God is able to orchestrate the universe we live in, I know I can trust Him to orchestrate my life.

20

The Pawn Shop

I wanted to have more children. I had wanted to be in love and be married into eternity. I never imagined that my marriage would end in divorce. I didn't realize that my marriage was unhealthy. Frank was up front about the trouble he had dealing with anger. He would often talk about going to anger management classes, but in our eleven years of marriage, he never did attend any classes. There were a couple times he went in for marriage counseling with me at the churches we attended. They would give us a test, and we would always pass on paper. It was hard to put a finger on the problem. One of the problems was his anger and his pattern of dealing with life. I don't think he knew that his way of living was abusive towards those he lived with. I know he was never fully honest with anyone. I don't think he was even honest with himself.

The last marriage counseling session we had with Pastor Tim and Rebecca ended the same as the rest. We both left with good advice, but I was the only one to follow it. I faithfully attended Cindy Sprague's Tuesday night classes on domestic abuse while Frank did nothing.

When I left him in April and moved into my own apartment, I was still hoping we would reconcile. I considered myself "separated." Even though I found out he had been using drugs and had cheated on me, I felt God could fix it. Even though I had put a restraining order on him when I left because I was afraid of him, I still thought there was going to be a miracle and everything would turn out right. I guess I was the typical spouse of an abuser.

By September, I was starting to realize the marriage was not going to be miraculously saved. Weeks would go by without getting a text from Frank and when I did get a text, it had nothing to do with us reconciling. I was in a safe place, I was no longer afraid, but I was hurt. I was starting to really realize that I had been rejected.

Rejection—what to do with that emotion? I could let my mind spin, trying to figure out how and why I wasn't good enough for my husband. But I didn't want to go there. Maybe I was beautiful enough, maybe I was loving enough, maybe I was sexy enough. Maybe I was a very good wife, and he just had his own personal problems. I couldn't afford to beat myself up emotionally. My heart was breaking, and it affected me physically, mentally, and emotionally.

I felt lonely for the first time in my life. I felt rejected, and I felt like nobody wanted or needed me. I found myself getting depressed. I was feeling more tired every day, and I would bounce back from feelings of deep sadness to aggressive anger. At night, I would lay on my bed and look up at the ceiling. Suddenly a wave of deep sadness would hit me. I was sad that the marriage didn't last. I was sad I was losing someone I had loved so dearly. I would cry so hard that my heart would physically hurt. One night, I lay in bed and gently rubbed my chest. I said, "It's okay Rose. This pain won't last forever. You loved well, and this was out of your control. You have no choice but to trust God and be patient. It's okay to hurt."

By mid-September, I knew it was time to move towards getting divorced. I had no idea how to go about it. I had never really talked with anyone about how to get divorced. I figured I would just pray about it and do a little research. I was starting to really admire anyone who had been through a divorce. I don't care who's fault the divorce was; it's a painful experience to go through.

My emotions kept swinging from sadness to anger. I think I was grieving the death of our marriage. One day when I was feeling particularly angry, I decided on a whim to sell my wedding ring. I thought, *I'll just go to a pawn shop and sell my wedding ring. I don't need it anymore, and I'll use the money to get divorced.*

I drove down to the pawn shop, got out of my car, and started walking towards the door. The parking lot was empty but the "Open" sign was lit. *Good*, I thought, *I'm glad it's not busy because this might be harder than I think.* I hesitated and walked back to my car. I got in, closed the door, and took my wedding ring out of my pocket. I thought, *I guess I should take a minute to look at it one last time.* I didn't feel like getting sentimental. I didn't want to cry. I was angry, and I just wanted to get it over with. I looked through the car window towards the "Open" sign on the door. *Maybe I should wait. It's probably not a good idea to sell my wedding ring in anger. Maybe I should wait to sell it until I'm actually divorced.* I didn't want to wait. I was tired of all these emotions. I got back out of my car and walked purposefully to the front door. I reached out to open the door, and my body jerked. The door was locked! I stepped back and looked again at the sign in the window. It was lit up and it said, "Open." I cupped my hands on the side of my face and peered in through the tinted glass of the door. There wasn't anyone inside. *I guess they are closed but forgot to turn off the sign.*

I put my wedding ring back into my pocket and walked back to my car. I had to laugh. I guess it wasn't time to sell my ring. I sat there in my car for a few minutes and decided to pray. I said, "Thank you, Lord, for being with me. I don't like what I'm going through, but I have decided to trust you. Thank you that the store was closed. I will wait to sell my wedding ring until after I'm divorced. Please keep guiding me. Help me to be patient. You are a God of order. Help me to get through this."

CHAPTER

Justice Must Be Served!

JOURNAL ENTRY: 9/25/16

All I have, all I know, all I care about is my God. My Creator. The pure and gentle lover of my soul. Though all is stripped away from me, I still have Him. I can trust Him. He gives and takes away. I don't want anything in my life to be above Him. His grace on me is enough.

It had been five months since I left Frank. At the beginning, I counted the days. I thought he was going to go get counseling, ask for my forgiveness, and we could possibly work things out. I remember mentioning this to Cindy Sprague at one of the Tuesday night classes. Her response surprised me. She said, "Don't hold your breath." She was right.

At the beginning, Frank denied everything. But after only a few months, his girlfriend had posted pics of the two of them together in Hawaii with the status, "In a Relationship." Although I went through a range of emotions, as the summer wound down, I began to have a peace in my heart about divorcing Frank. The problem was that I had no idea how to go about getting a divorce.

I was able to visit with family at least once a month. In September, I went to Greenville to spend the weekend with my brother Jared and his family. Jared had always been my best friend. He was proud of me for leaving Frank. I was open with him about everything. One evening as we finished a lovely meal, I told him I was just taking one day at a time. I was trusting God to guide me, and I felt like I should divorce Frank. I told him that the problem was I didn't know how to go about it. I started to cry. I was overcome with emotion.

Jared stood up and grabbed me by both hands. He was shaking. He looked straight into my eyes and with a restrained voice he said, "Justice must be served!" Although he had tears in his eyes, he seemed very angry. I don't know if it was anger or sorrow, but he was very intense. He told me to go back home and look for the very best lawyer in town. He said money was no object, and he and his wife Amélie wanted to pay for everything. He said, "Be sure to take your time and find the very best divorce lawyer in town. And when you do, have them contact me and we will take care of any costs."

I hugged him and thanked him and cried. I was happy for their help. It was a great relief to not have to worry about the cost, and it was also a great relief to not have to go through it alone. Even though I would go home and find the lawyer by myself and go to the meetings by myself and sign the divorce papers by myself, their act of giving made it feel like they would be there with me. Maybe this is what it means to "bear one another's burdens."

22

No Contact

I remember the victim's advocate at the courthouse suggesting that I request a "no contact order" to be included with the restraining order I was asking to be put on Frank. At the time, I told her I wanted my husband to be able to contact me in case he was planning to change. I felt the space would be enough for him to realize he was being abusive. Maybe he would go for counseling and want to save our marriage.

Looking back, I regret that I made an allowance for text messages. His texts to me were confusing and unpredictable. This made every day a little harder to get through. Some days I would glance at my phone hoping to see his name pop up. But as the days turned into weeks and the weeks into months, I started to dread receiving a text from him.

Frank continued to be abusive toward me, even from a safe distance. His texts would alternate from apologizing for hurting me to lying about any involvement with another woman to blaming me for giving up on the marriage. I was exhausted.

By fall I was ready to file for divorce. I wanted it to be as quick and easy as possible. I was hoping for a "friendly divorce," but I couldn't even imagine what that would look like. I just knew I didn't want to hate Frank, and I no longer wanted to be afraid of him.

I decided I wanted to have a phone conversation with Frank. I had not heard his voice since the night before I left him. I sent him a text and asked if he would like to have a phone conversation with me. He agreed that he would, so we set it up for him to call me at 9:00 p.m. on Tuesday night.

At 8:45 I walked out of my apartment and went downstairs to the swimming pool area to wait for his call. I was excited to hear his voice. I kicked off my sandals and sat at the edge of the pool, in the same place I did many evenings. I enjoyed gently kicking my feet in the water. It was relaxing. The sky was getting dark, and the stars were starting to appear. The evening air was warm, and it felt good to have my feet in the water. As I waited for the phone call, I drew in a deep breath of air. I felt comfortable. From where I sat, I could see the soft light coming from my apartment living room. It looked inviting. I was beginning to love my new home.

Nine o'clock came and went without a call from Frank.

At 9:20 I sent him a text: "Do you want to call me?" He texted back: "I'm afraid to talk to you for some reason." I appreciated his honesty. I texted: "It's okay. I promise to keep the conversation light and short. If either one of us feels uncomfortable, we can just say goodbye."

At 9:30 my phone rang. I looked at the screen, and the name "Patricia" came up. My mother-in-law?! I felt scared. She hadn't called or spoken to me since April 11 and for a moment I was afraid to answer the phone. I pressed the answer button and said, "Hello?"

Frank said, "Hi Rose."

"Oh, thank God!" I said. "I thought your mom was calling me!"

We both laughed and chatted with each other for about ten minutes. We talked about the pets, and I talked about the scripture I had read about Pleiades and Orion. The conversation was light and short, but it felt good to me. Maybe we could have more phone conversations to help remove the fear, hurt, and anger. Maybe it could help make the divorce process easier. Maybe it would help both of us to get on with our individual futures.

The following week, I sent Frank a text asking him if he would like to have another phone conversation. He texted: "Okay, on Tuesday night if I can." The phone call never happened. Weeks went by without receiving any texts from Frank. I had saved every text we had written to each other since April 11, and as I went back to read them, I realized the conversations were completely unproductive and, in fact, very unhealthy for me.

I decided to delete all the texts. It wasn't easy to do, but it felt right. I had to move forward. If God wanted to miraculously save our marriage, He could, but I had run out of ideas of how that would work.

You're doing great! Don't be so hard on yourself. You're going through a huge transition. You'll be single soon and with your maiden name again. Who knows? Maybe you will find love again and marry. For now, buckle down and finish the tasks at hand.

Divorce. Get a new name. Have a clean heart. Be in right fellowship with God. Have faith. Become debt-free. Build savings. Plan for retirement. Get health insurance.

For now, enjoy your cozy home. Enjoy your son. Enjoy your friends and family. Enjoy the four seasons. Eat, drink, rest, play, work, exercise and learn something new. Maybe become fluent in French? God is with you.

CHAPTER

The Divorce

JOURNAL ENTRY: 10/7/16

My divorce consultation with Tori McMillian was moved up two weeks. Went peacefully and smoothly. Could be divorced and an Evans again within two weeks! I'm actually excited.

JOURNAL ENTRY: 10/9/16

A three-stranded cord is not easily broken. For sure. I regret not doing my part in the marriage of nurturing the third part of our strand. Our relationship with God. Divorce is not easily done.

This morning I awoke to a gift from my son. He drove up to Franklin last weekend with some friends and brought back a gift for me! It was a bottle of red wine, a dark chocolate orange, a small green glass candle holder with an Irish clover candle, a box of Guinness chocolates (with two eaten), and a pack of British pub coasters. The note inside said, "Sometimes I'll talk to my mom and I'll just pause and wonder how I could possibly ever love someone more than this woman."

I love that young man! I will save the wine to celebrate becoming an Evans again.

JOURNAL ENTRY: 10/10/16

As the day approaches to sign the divorce papers I find myself confused. I'm excited to be moving past the hurt and rejection, but unsure. I'm questioning if I should forgive and allow the marriage to be mended. But how could I ever trust him again? I have zero interest in living with him at his mother's house and zero interest in putting up with his anger and lack of purpose. I no longer wish to be attached to him. I suppose I also broke the vow that I made to stay with him for richer or poorer, for better or worse.

I will keep my eyes on Jesus. I pray for a soft heart without fear.

Today at work I smelled the familiar smell of infection in my sinuses. It's probably related to the infected tooth that is finally scheduled to be pulled out. Instead of panic and warning at the smell that something is terribly wrong, I told myself, "Oh, it's just the infection."

Why do women stay with abusers? Well, along with all the other documented reasons, I believe they stay because the 'red flag' warnings have become familiar. It's very dangerous.

I am ready to be divorced. I will no longer tolerate his abuse. Not even by text. I am ready to remove my abuser from my life like a rotten tooth. PULL IT OUT!!!

Got a text from Frank tonight. It said, "Yes, I signed it." My heart physically hurts.

I slept well last night. I had dreams of going to youth camp. I woke to a beautiful golden-red sunrise and thought of the words from the old song "Because He Lives." It feels good to be able to let go of fear and grab onto hope.

I woke to another beautiful sunrise this morning. Every night I sleep well and wake up refreshed. I dream about things I don't know. I feel like the Lord is telling me things in my dreams and teaching me.

I am blessed. I have been rescued out of a bad situation. The Lord has been sweet to me and very protective.

Today I will sign the divorce papers, and I'm ready. I'm ready to be Rose Evans again, and I'm ready to belong to the Lord. I am grateful and happy.

Today I signed the same divorce paper that Frank signed. I saw his signature. Maybe I'll be divorced soon.

Anyway, I cried.

24

Let's Go Shopping!

I hate the word "divorce." I always have. It's an ugly word, and it leaves a horrible taste in one's heart. My divorce only took a week to become final, but during that week, my daily routine went back to pushing myself from one moment to the next. While I would be showering, I would be saying to myself, "Next, you are going to eat some breakfast and then brush your teeth." And then I would get dressed and go to work. I did the best I could to stay positive. I was heartbroken and disappointed. I found it ironic that the very reason I had waited until I was thirty-eight to get married was because of how much I hated divorce.

But here I was, walking through my worst fear. I felt like I was in a dream. Whenever I was alone, I would cry. It was so hard to eat food and even harder to let it digest. My whole self was upset. I began to lose more weight. One night

I went to a birthday party but then just left early. I wanted to go home so I could be sad, angry, and lonely in private.

I received a text from Frank. It said, "Thanks a lot for leaving me with the phone bill and taxes and the animals. I hate you. Thanks a lot."

I couldn't react or respond. I simply deleted the text.

I have company staying with me this weekend, and I know that my divorce is in the works and soon I will no longer be married to Frank. God is gentle. He knows that without distraction, this would be hard for me.

Still, I have no privacy as I am about to read the email from my lawyer stating that, as of today, my divorce is final.

I will tell Charlie first, then mom, then Abby, then I'll text Leah, Jared, and Jo. And then I will change my name on Facebook and post, "My name is Rose Evans!"

It just so happened that my stepmother, Abby, was spending the weekend with me when I received the email from my lawyer that my divorce was final. It was probably good that I wasn't alone. I was tired of being so sad. After breakfast I said to Abby, "Well, I'm officially divorced so I was wondering if you would like to go with me to the pawn shop. I need to sell my wedding ring, and I want to use the money to get some decorations for my house—Christmas is coming!"

Abby smiled and said, "Well then, let's go!"

As eager as I was to sell my wedding ring a month earlier, when it came time to actually sell it, it was not an easy thing to do. I could have chosen anger to make it feel easier, but I did not want to have that toxic emotion inside of me. If I chose sorrow, I wouldn't have sold the ring at all. I would have kept it in a drawer so I could pull it out anytime I wanted to stroll down memory lane. But I didn't want to do that either. What good is it to spend today crying about yesterday? I decided to choose acceptance. I did not like the way things turned out, but I trusted God.

After I sold the ring, I walked over to Abby and started to cry. She reached out and pulled me close to her and held me in a good long hug. I took my time and just let myself cry. Then I pulled myself away, wiped my eyes, and said, "Come on! We have some shopping to do!"

25

Baseball

Fall was in the air, and with it came a sense of hopefulness. Everything seemed crisp and clean. The air was fresh, and the sky was a clear deep blue. I was acutely aware of all the colors of the leaves this year. The deep reds, the burnt orange, and even the yellow leaves were so bright they almost hurt my eyes. It felt good to no longer be in a place of waiting and wondering if my marriage would be saved. I was ready to move on, but my heart was still hurting. I decided to send Frank one last text. I badly wanted some closure.

JOURNAL ENTRY: 10/31/16

Me: "Hi, Frank. I just wanted to let you know that the divorce is final so we are no longer married. I never thought we would divorce, and I'm sorry that we both had to go through

*this. I'm sorry for my part in its failure. I wish
you the best for your life, and I have very fond
memories of our times together."*

*Frank: "Me too. It's the worst thing that's
happened in my life! I still can't believe it. I
hope the best for you also Rose; hope we can be
friends later down the road. I love you and will
miss you so very much. Take care."*

The texts didn't give me the feeling of closure I was
hoping for. I had to trust that God was in control and that
He cared for me and for Frank. I could trust God with my
future. I decided I would just keep living one day at a time,
moment by moment if I had to.

A few days later, I called my mom to talk with her about
the Cubs winning the World Series. We both love baseball.
It's a game of incredible athletic skill, but it's also a game
that includes odds. That's what I love most about it. "It's not
over till it's over!" My mom told me she had a dream that
she caught a homerun ball and she kept it! We talked about
how wonderful it would be to go to Wrigley Field together
someday to watch the Cubs play.

After the phone call, I was thinking about odds and physics
and how strange this life is. I started to wonder how much I
really mattered to anyone. I was sitting on my bed, listening to
some music that I had downloaded to my phone. I was listening
through my earbuds so the music was very clear and beautiful.
An acoustic version of U2's song "Every Breaking Wave" came

on, and I started to feel sad. I decided I would go outside to listen to the song while looking up at the stars.

I went out the front door and down the steps to the grassy area just in front of my apartment. It was pretty late, and I didn't need to go far to see the stars. Anyway, I just wanted to stand there and look at the stars and listen to the sad song and feel sorry for myself. Maybe God would see me and feel sorry for me too.

As I stood there, listening to the song, I looked up into the night sky. I was looking at the universe. The stars were beautiful as usual. I thought to myself:

> Yes, God sees me
> Yes, I matter
> Yes, He feels bad for me
> Yes, He will do more great things
> Yes, there is hope!

Just then I saw another fat shooting star! It shot straight across the sky from east to west. It looked like a huge fireball speeding across the dark sky. A long bright trail of red, orange, and gold sparkles followed it. Then as quickly as it appeared, it disappeared. I could not believe the timing of it.

I walked back up the stairs and into my warm apartment. I was still thinking about physics and baseball and odds and the timing of that shooting star. I knew I could trust God with my life. Life is a little like baseball. It isn't over 'till it's over, and it's God who controls the odds.

26

CHAPTER

The Sunstones

JOURNAL ENTRY: 11/9/16

Frank sent me a text today. It said, "Would you please remove the restraining order? Hope your day is good," followed by a smiley face. Weird. I sent him a text back that said, "I do not feel comfortable removing the restraining order. Why would you ask that? It takes time for a person to heal from the pain of learning that the person they trusted is not trustworthy." There was no reply.

I had thought that once the divorce was over, I would be able to move on and start feeling better. But I was actually starting to feel worse. Frank's texts were still confusing me, and I was still afraid of running into him in town. The finality of divorce was a heavy reality for me to really take in. I started to lose weight again and felt exhausted every day. The peace and comfort I felt from God at the beginning was not as strong. I felt like God wasn't close to me anymore. And I felt very, very sad.

I knew I needed to continue on moment by moment. I was hoping that by now I would be stronger than that, but the waves of emotion were overwhelming me. I was grateful for my consistent daily routine, including my job. My coworkers were supportive of me. They left me alone when I wanted to be left alone, and they talked with me when I wanted to talk. They even shared their lunch with me when I forgot to bring something to eat.

My clients were also supportive. I had no choice but to let them know I was going through a difficult time in my personal life. Some of my clients told me they would be praying for me. Some of them actually prayed for me before leaving the salon! It was challenging to stay focused and professional during a crisis, but God gave me grace, and my work continued to prosper. My clients were more of an encouragement than they even knew.

JOURNAL ENTRY: 11/11/16

I love my clients! Today, Matt Steinberg came in for a haircut, and he gave me a gift. It's really not like him. He is a private man and reserved. He seems like a healthy man in a healthy marriage. He knows I love to find and collect stones, so when he was out hiking, he found some sunstones and polished them and gave them to me as a gift! This was so awesome. It was just what I needed today.

I looked up the sunstone meaning: "Sunstone is a powerful stone used in crystal energy work for dispelling fears and phobias of all kinds. It is also a leadership stone and brings leadership qualities to its wearer. In addition to dispelling fears and phobias, sunstone is also used to decrease stress and lift depression."

I was determined to get healthy again. I was tired of being tired and tired of crying. I continued to write in my journal almost every evening. It helped to put my thoughts down on paper. I was grieving the loss of my marriage, the loss of my husband, and the loss of my pets. The journal helped me to stay grounded. When my thoughts would race, writing them down usually helped me to change my perspective.

JOURNAL ENTRY: 11/13/16 8:45pm

Tonight there is a full moon. A Super Moon! I can honestly say I do not like the moon tonight. It's too bright, it hurts my eyes, and I feel like it's driving me crazy!

I can't breathe today, I can't stop crying, and my blood pressure is high. I feel like I'm one step away from death or insanity!

Karma . . . they say it's a bitch. You know, I once lived a dual life. I lied to everyone I knew, and everyone who loved me, in order to conceal a habitual lifestyle. I had chosen to hurt any man who showed an interest in me. Yep . . . I had sex with many a married man with no concern for the innocent spouse. In fact, my son was conceived by a man not married to me. The word says, "Do not be deceived, God will not be mocked. Whatsoever a man soweth, that also will he reap." And guess what? I'm reaping the whirlwind! The pain is almost unbearable. It feels like it could kill me.

But guess what else? I also sowed humility, confession, and repentance! And God made a way for me to be pardoned. Through Jesus. His sacrifice was perfect and complete.

I will get through this by God's grace, and the claws of the enemy cannot grasp me! It is for freedom that we have been set free and whom the Lord sets free is free indeed!

I had to forgive Frank, and I had to forgive myself. I had to be patient with the process of grief. I had to be patient with the process of acceptance.

The sunstones were a beautiful gift. Although they didn't help to dispel my fears and phobias, or lift my depression or decrease my stress, they did remind me that someone was thinking of me and genuinely cared about my well-being. And they did teach me to never underestimate the long-lasting impact of a small act of kindness.

> *I had to forgive Frank, and I had to forgive myself. I had to be patient with the process of grief. I had to be patient with the process of acceptance.*

27

Grief

I don't even want to write in this journal tonight. I'm constantly tired and so sad lately. I cry whenever I can so I can get through this part of the process. Humans are fragile. I've been hurt bad. I want to heal well.

Tonight, I can't stop crying for my pets. I loved them and had to leave them behind. I was counseled to get out and leave the pets. It's true.

At least they are happy with each other. I wish I could have Daisy and Lady here with me. My heart is so broken. I wonder if I will be able to love an animal or a person again. I hope so. I have to trust God.

I was beginning to feel more and more comfortable in my new apartment. And although my daily routine seemed to be working for me, moving on to a new life chapter was not a quick or easy task. Sometimes the sadness would overtake me. This usually happened in the evenings. I guess I had spent all day moving forward and staying positive, and then there was that time between dinner and bedtime when I would just cry. I had heard somewhere that you shouldn't fight grief, but I couldn't afford to be crying all day. And I had heard that anger was also a part of grief, but I couldn't afford to be angry at work so I grieved in the evenings.

For a while, every night after dinner I would walk out onto my balcony and look out at the evening sky. Sometimes the sun was just setting and a few birds were still flitting around the bushes. Sometimes the sun had just set, and I could see the first few stars twinkling in the pale blue sky. Sometimes it was dark, and I could see the reflection of the moon over the grassy area just below my balcony.

I would lean on the edge of the balcony and just breathe. I would allow the thoughts to come, and I would either feel sorrow or rage. Sometimes my heart would be so heavy that I would just stand there and sob. It was not the time to try to

> *It was not the time to try to figure out who did what and why; it was just a time to allow my broken heart to hurt.*

figure out who did what and why; it was just a time to allow my broken heart to hurt.

Sometimes I would stand there and turn my face to the south. I would shout out towards Frank's house and ask him why he did what he did. I would look over the hills and imagine my angry words hitting his ears. All of this felt like grief to me, so I just went with it. I didn't know how long these intense emotions would last, but it felt healthy and I just wanted to get through it.

Frank's birthday was coming up, and we were no longer married. It felt so strange. There was no closure and no explanations. I wasn't really sure how to move forward. I hadn't received any texts from Frank since the divorce. The finality of it all had to set in. I guess it would take time. I decided I would send him a text on his birthday. It was probably more for me than for him.

JOURNAL ENTRY: 11/17/16, Frank's Birthday

I sent Frank a text this morning. I wanted to say 'Happy Birthday' and that I was thinking of him. A response didn't matter to me. I have the choice to keep my heart happy.

9:02 am, my text: "Happy Birthday, Frank!! Thinking of you and I hope you have a wonderful day."

Frank's response: "Thanks, appreciate that. Have a good day!"

I had heard that after losing a loved one, the first year of grief is the hardest. They say you need to get through a year of "firsts." First Easter without them, first Fourth of July, etc. This was the first birthday in eleven years that I would not be celebrating with this man. Sending the text made me feel pretty good. I've been accused of being sentimental. I think I'm just human. I decided I would allow myself a few moments every evening to be either sad or angry, then I would move on. I also gave myself permission to go through a year of "firsts." I wanted to accept the reality of the fact that my husband chose drugs and another woman over me. I wanted to accept the fact that God pulled me out of that relationship, and I wanted to accept the fact that my marriage was over but I needed time to grieve. So I decided I would just keep moving forward. God would be with me through all the firsts of this year.

JOURNAL ENTRY: 11/17/16 8:05pm

Klove's verse for today was Jeremiah 29:11, "For I know the plans I have for you declares The Lord, plans to prosper you and not to harm you, plans to give you hope and a future."

This made me cry and pray for more faith. I said, "I trust you, Lord."

28

My Name Is Rose Evans!

A month after the divorce was final, I went down to the social security office and had my name changed back to Rose Evans. It felt strange and wonderful to have my maiden name back. Maybe marriage just wasn't for me. I spent some time in the waiting room of the social security office developing a new signature. It didn't feel right signing my name the same way I did for years before marrying Frank.

I left the social security office and drove straight to the DMV. I parked my car and looked through the papers they gave me for my name change. I spent a few minutes perfecting the new signature. I came up with a pretty scribbled version of "Rose Evans," and I liked it. After the DMV I had to go to the post office. Suddenly, I realized how much work it was going to take to get my name changed everywhere. Maybe that's why so many women don't change their names after a divorce.

After spending time at the social security office, the DMV, and the post office, I realized that it would take longer than one day to change my name. I was going to have to make the rest of the changes as they came up. It was my day off and the weather was beautiful. I wanted to relax and just enjoy being Rose Evans again.

I drove to the YMCA to go for a swim. When I got into the pool, I resolved to spend as much time as I wanted in the water. Instead of swimming laps, I went over to the open swim area and just played in the water. I did handstands and back floats and swam under the water like a mermaid. The afternoon sun was shining in through the windows so, from time to time, I would hold onto the edge of the pool and just allow the beautiful sunshine to pour over me. Then I would let myself fall back into the water and totally submerge myself. When I was under the water, I would look up at the surface and remember getting baptized. I felt wonderful.

JOURNAL ENTRY: 11/21/16

After running all over town I went to the YMCA and swam and played in the perfect waters of the pool for over an hour.

Now I'm at home making a lasagna dinner with fresh garlic bread and Malbec merlot wine. Music is on, the night is perfectly clean,

fresh, and cool, and tears are streaming down
my face.

I feel like I felt when I was ten years old and my
dad hadn't left yet, and I was not yet a woman.
I felt perfect then, and I feel perfect now.

It felt good to be finally moving forward. That night after dinner I posted on Facebook, "My name is Rose Evans!"

29

A Time Of Thanksgiving

They say, "Time flies when you're having fun!" I learned from experience that the opposite is also true. Time crawls when you're going through a hard time. I'm sure that from an outsider's perspective, it looked like I moved very quickly. After all, I left Frank, put a restraining order on him, and moved into a new apartment all in one day. But from my perspective, from the moment I learned about Frank's drug use and affair, time slowed down to a painful crawl.

I'm so grateful for the wisdom and guidance I received from Cindy Sprague. I'm also grateful that Rebecca sent me to Cindy's weekly classes on domestic abuse. It was in those classes I was able to see I was trapped in an unhealthy and abusive relationship. The moment I recognized I needed to get out was the moment time slowed down for me. I used Cindy's advice of going "moment by moment" when I needed to, and that helped me to get through the early days.

I used to look out the bedroom window of my new apartment every morning. I was watching the trees to see if we were coming into a new season. When I first moved into the apartment, the trees were bare. There may have been small buds growing, but to me they looked like bare trees. Little by little I began to see buds. It seemed to take forever for me to see flowers, and then finally the trees were full with green leaves. By summer, I was no longer going "moment by moment" and before long, the leaves changed into the beautiful colors of fall.

Thanksgiving was coming, and I was no longer married to Frank. I decided I wanted to spend this Thanksgiving alone with my son. The apartment was already starting to look very festive. I had purchased a few Christmas items with the money I got from selling my wedding ring, so I decided to decorate for Christmas early. Why wait? If I wanted to set up my house for Christmas before Thanksgiving, who was going to stop me? I had been through enough grief. I was ready for the holidays to come! I bought a white table runner with embroidered snowflakes that I put on the dining room table. It looked wonderful against the wood grain. I also bought a beautiful wooden bowl that I filled up with walnuts. It looked good on the table too. Other new items showed up around the apartment. A row of decorative wood-cut pine trees and a tall wooden nutcracker wearing a very regal outfit of sparkling blue and white. Next to the nutcracker stood a majestic looking St. Nick. He was wearing a long, sparkling blue and white robe, and he was holding a small pine tree in his hand. All of these items were bringing a new joy into the apartment and into my heart.

Thanksgiving Day was beautiful. It was cool and cloudy with just a light mist of rain. Charlie was playing his guitar while I prepared the meal. I had a few small candles lit, some on the dining room table and a couple on the kitchen counter. It was a perfect day, and the apartment was filled with wonderful smells. A small turkey breast, fully cooked, was warming in the oven. I made mashed potatoes, gravy, green beans, and stuffing. I put out cranberry sauce, fresh rolls with butter, and, of course, a tray of black and green olives with sweet and dill pickles.

My heart was filling with joy and new hope. As we sat down for dinner, I asked Charlie if I could say the prayer.

He smiled and said, "Of course."

"Dear Lord, I thank you for what you have done, for what you are doing, and for what you are planning to do. Thank you for being so good to us. Thank you for your love. Amen."

The sun broke through the clouds once or twice during the meal. Of course, the west window blinds were wide open. I love sunlight. When the sunshine came in, the table looked lovely. My son's face was also beautiful. He looked happy and content. When the clouds covered the sunlight, the warm glow of the candles took over. There was one moment during the meal when I couldn't help but let the tears flow down my face.

Charlie noticed and said, "Oh, Mom. I'm so sorry. I didn't mean to make you cry." He thought he made cry by choosing to play a song by Enya on the stereo. He quickly switched to a different song.

I smiled and wiped my tears and said, "It's okay. I just have to cry sometimes."

Truth is that I cried because the song by Enya reminded me of all of the great times Charlie and I had together during his childhood. I felt bad for my choice in marrying Frank, and I felt bad for the stress my marriage put on my son. But here we were, enjoying a simple Thanksgiving feast together. We were both healthy and safe, and I felt as if I could feel God's presence with us. God was with us, and that was enough for me.

JOURNAL ENTRY: 11/24/16
Thanksgiving Day

Today marks the one-year anniversary of what I didn't know at the time would be the last time I would ever have to experience the "cycle of abuse" from my ex-husband. Last Thanksgiving, he had an explosive outrage at our family dinner, witnessed (and forgiven) by all except for my son and me. It was on that horrible drive home (horrible only for us since my ex-husband had already moved on from the "explosion phase" to the "honeymoon phase") that I determined in my heart I would never tolerate this behavior again. My son was the first one to encourage me to separate from Frank to show him that this behavior was unacceptable. In my heart that day I said, "Never again."

As I got ready for bed that night, a Bible verse kept coming to my mind. All I could think of was the first three words: "this poor man." So I Googled "this poor man," and Psalm 34:6 came up. I decided to look the verse up in my Bible instead of using my phone app. I snuggled up against the pillows of my bed and opened up my Bible where the ribbon bookmark was last left. I guess I had inadvertently placed the bookmark in the middle of the Bible. It just so happened to be marking Psalm 34! I got excited to read the passage. It felt like the Lord Himself was just waiting for me to read these words with Him. The passage was as true for me as it was for David when he wrote it. It said, "This poor man cried, and the Lord heard him, and saved him out of all his troubles."

I sat back on my pillows and thought to myself, *Today I am most grateful for my God.* This poor soul cried out for help and was delivered. I was not only rescued and removed from danger and abuse but I

> *This poor soul cried out for help and was delivered. I was not only rescued and removed from danger and abuse but I was also given peace, hope, and healing.*

was also given peace, hope, and healing. Today I can smile, breathe and live.

People marvel at my "strength." The truth is that it was only by allowing myself to be weak, hopeless, and confused and aware of my own mortality that I found strength. I realized I had nothing to do with being created and I have nothing to do with when and how I die. One night I looked to the stars and believed in the Invisible God who made me. I saw Him as perfect, good, loving, and trustworthy. I cast my soul at His feet, broken and humble.

It was God who rescued me—not only this time but every time throughout my whole life. I realized I am not my own but His. Yet He gave me my life, and I am permitted to guard it. I am, and will always be, His first.

30

The Christmas Tree

Christmas has always been special to Charlie. I believe it is his favorite time of the year. During his childhood, I often marveled at how excited he would get at the first signs of the coming season. He would notice before I did that the city had put up the row of large candy canes, Christmas trees, and lanterns that alternated each streetlight along the main road in Fairview. I was glad to see I hadn't passed down my negative feelings about the holiday. In fact, it was after he was born that I decided I would change my attitude about Christmas for his sake.

When I was young, I also loved Christmastime. But after my parents got divorced, those feelings changed for me. Christmas was strange after the divorce. We no longer had a father in the home, money was tight, and it was weird and uncomfortable to celebrate the holidays in two separate homes. By my teenage years, I just started to ignore the season altogether. Sure, I would participate in holiday events, but my heart wasn't in it. By the time I was in my twenties, I didn't even bother to buy a Christmas tree.

But that all changed after Charlie was born. My perspective on life itself changed, and I am thankful for that. I realize now that I could have changed my attitude years earlier and saved myself a lot of unnecessary heartache.

It's interesting that the thing I once so desperately tried to push away was now the very thing I was eagerly grabbing onto. I was falling in love with the holidays all over again. My apartment was already decorated for Christmas on Thanksgiving Day! This was a fun and beautiful time for me. I decided that from now on, I wanted to belong to the group that set up their Christmas tree on Thanksgiving weekend!

I didn't have time to wallow in my sorrows. I couldn't afford to let my divorce ruin the rest of my life. God was with me, and He seemed to be moving forward. So I just kept taking one step at a time.

Four days after Thanksgiving, Charlie and I went out to buy a Christmas tree. It was fun! It didn't take us long to find the perfect tree. In fact, we bought the first tree we saw on the lot. We brought it back to the apartment, and I decorated it while Charlie watched a Christmas movie on TV. It was fun shopping for the tree, getting it into the house, and putting on the lights, but when it came time to put on the ornaments, I hesitated.

I knew I would have to open up another box from our storage unit—the Christmas box. The last time I saw the contents of that box was two years ago when Frank and I moved into his mother's house. I figured it would be emotional, but I knew God was with me. Somehow, I managed to survive opening that first kitchen box seven months earlier. And the first item I opened that day was the communion glass from our wedding day! God was with me that day, and I dealt with it. I cried, thanked God for the good times, trusted Him for the rest, and I let it go. I was sure the Christmas box would be fine, so I opened it up.

Each ornament was carefully wrapped in tissue. This would be fun! I knew all of my favorite ornaments from Charlie's childhood were in that box, so I just picked up an ornament and unwrapped the tissue. I couldn't believe it. The first ornament I opened was a bride and groom that said, "First Christmas"! I lowered my hands and sat down next to the box. I looked at the ornament in my hands. It was a bride and groom. I looked at the box full of wrapped ornaments and just knew there were lots of cute ornaments in that box with sweet memories.

I looked up at the tree. It was full of colored lights. I took a lot of time placing the lights just so, and it looked perfect. But it needed ornaments! I could hear the Christmas movie on the TV, and the apartment felt festive. I had to move on. I decided I would just open each ornament in the box and when I came across any that made me feel sad, I would just set them to the side and deal with them later. I had a tree to decorate!

By the end of the evening, the tree looked perfect. I stood up and looked at the empty Christmas box. Beside the box lay a pile of tissue paper and several ornaments that held memories of my life with Frank. I gathered all of it and walked over to the trash can. Tears flowed down my face. I paused and said a prayer. I thanked God for all He had done, all He was doing, and all He was going to do. I said a prayer of faith. I felt sad, but I was learning to trust in God's goodness. I also said a prayer for Frank. I hadn't heard from him since his birthday. I prayed God would be near to him as he might be hurting too.

Then I made two cups of hot chocolate and loaded the top with mini marshmallows. I handed one to Charlie and snuggled up next to him to watch the rest of the Christmas movie. I glanced over to the Christmas tree. It was beautiful. Each ornament held a special memory. I glanced back to my son's face. He was smiling. No words were necessary. My heart was content.

31

Choose Joy

The days and weeks were getting easier to get through. My new routine was working well for me. I had set up a pretty structured schedule. I would go to bed at the same time every night and wake up at the same time every morning. When it was time to eat, I made healthy choices. I stayed hydrated and swam laps at the YMCA twice a week. When it was time to work, I worked, and when it was time to rest, I rested. I was still "going moment by moment" in a way, but it was different than when I first left Frank. Back then, I had to "go moment by moment" just to stay alive. Now I was "going moment by moment" by choice. I was grateful for God's presence in my life, and I wanted to honor Him every moment of my day.

A change was taking place in my mind as well. I began to realize I could choose to cooperate with God's guidance. I believed that God loved me and could speak to me through the scriptures, so every morning I would have my cup of coffee with the Lord. I would open my Bible and just read it. Sometimes the passages would jump off the page right into my heart, and sometimes I would just read a story and ponder its meaning. It seemed like reading the scriptures helped my mind to catch up with what my spirit already knew—that I could trust God and that I could choose joy.

JOURNAL ENTRY: 12/3/16

It's Christmastime and I have decided to enjoy the Christmas lights. If I see a family or a couple, I have decided to feel happy for them. I played a board game tonight with Jacob. It was fun! Surprisingly, since I hate games. I have played two games in two months. A new record for me, and I enjoyed both times!

I have decided to celebrate life. All of it. The good, the bad, the hard, or the impossible. There are seasons in life—each one should be cherished. I am content because God loves me. Not for what I've done or not done. He just loves me, and that's enough.

CHAPTER

New Traditions

As I prepared for the holidays, my thoughts went back thirty years to the Christmas I spent in Holland. Those were some of the best days of my life. I was young and hopeful, and the time I spent there shaped my heart. I found it interesting that after all these years, I was remembering those days. It seemed the more I allowed myself to let go of the things that were hurting me, the more I would rediscover the things that gave me joy.

When I lived in Holland, I got to experience the Dutch tradition of "Sinterklaas." It was so fun and exciting to experience a tradition brand new to me but centuries old to those I was living with. I will never forget the excitement of both children and adults as I stood in the marketplace, watching a parade of "Schwarte Pete's" pass by throwing small gingerbread cookies out to the crowd of shoppers. I was standing inside a bookstore at the time, when the door opened and I heard a commotion and saw a stream of tiny cookies land on the floor by my feet. I asked my friend to tell me what was happening. She said, "Oh, let's go outside and watch . . . Sinterklaas is coming!"

Apparently, every year on December 6, Sinterklaas sails by ship from Spain to Holland. He is accompanied by his helper Schwarte Pete, and his white horse is also on the ship. When he arrives in Amsterdam, it's a big deal! He gets on his white horse and begins his journey to deliver special treats to all the Dutch children. On the evening of December 5, the children need to put their wooden shoes out by the front door. They should also leave a few carrots for Sinterklaas' horse. If they have been good all year, Sinterklaas will leave a few treats and gifts. Schwarte Pete has a big bag, full of treats. If they aren't good, they will probably just receive a lump of coal. I received a special treat that I will always remember. It was a large dark chocolate bar in the shape of an "R" for Rose.

For a few years when Charlie was small, I had continued this tradition. But then it fell away. For some reason, this year I decided that Sinterklaas might want to come to our tiny apartment. So, on the evening of December 5, I pulled out my wooden shoes and put a few carrots inside. I told Charlie and his friend Jacob that they should be excited because Schwarte Pete might leave them some treats in the morning. Of course, Charlie is grown now, but he is a pretty good sport and was very sweet to tolerate whatever it was I was going through.

The next morning the doorbell rang. I asked Charlie to open the door as I thought that Schwarte Pete may have stopped by. He opened the front door and looked down to see the wooden shoes with a few broken carrot pieces inside, and next to the shoes were two brown bags tied with ribbon. One bag was for Charlie and the other for Jacob.

Charlie smiled and looked back at me and said, "You're the best." His bag had a box of mango tropical popsicles, Ferrero Rocher chocolates and a package of bacon. Jacob's bag had a box of macaroni & cheese, a box of butter, and a bag of sour gummy worm candies. Schwarte Pete's U.S. delivery was much different than what I had experienced in Holland, but Charlie seemed quite content. He paused to take a photo of the bag of goodies, opened up a popsicle, and walked into his room smiling. It's good to make new traditions or even to resurrect old ones. It's fun and it feels good.

33

CHAPTER

The Surgeon

It had been eight months since I walked out of Frank's life and put a restraining order on him. And it had been three months since I'd divorced him. One Sunday at church, I was walking past Rebecca and she stopped me and asked, "How are you doing, Rose?"

I smiled and said, "I'm doing pretty good!"

She smiled and hugged me and said, "Whom the Lord sets free is free indeed. You're free!"

I smiled at her and went on my way. Set free? Free indeed? I didn't feel very free. My heart still felt broken, and I felt very fragile going through ordinary everyday tasks. I pondered that statement for several days: *Whom the Lord sets free is free indeed.* The Lord did set me free. When I looked back, I could see that it was God who called out to me, and I responded by "going all in" and getting baptized on Easter

Sunday. When I looked back through my journal, I could see that it was God who pulled me out of an abusive marriage. God opened up the opportunity for me to attend Cindy Sprague's weekly classes on domestic abuse where I began to see that I was in a very unhealthy marriage. It was God who nudged me to look at my husband's phone texts to find out that he had been cheating on me with another woman. It was God who "parted the waters" and allowed me to leave an abusive husband, put a restraining order on him, and move into a new apartment all in one day. And it was God who picked me up and set me free! So why didn't I feel free?

I guess it takes time to adjust to freedom. It takes time and a little work. I had spent the summer separating all financial ties to Frank. I took myself off of our joint bank account. I "sold" the truck we owned together so my name would be off of the title. We went through an awkward conference call with our cell phone provider to get separate accounts and finally, thanks to my brother Jared's help, I divorced Frank.

> *I guess it takes time to adjust to freedom.*

If the Lord is setting you free from something, you have to trust Him, and you have to cooperate with Him. You have to do your part, but you also have to let God do His part. I won't lie. It's painful, but it's worth it. Sometimes temporary pain leads to eventual relief. Sort of like if you get a toe dislocated from jumping off a fence wearing wet shoes. I did that once. I had climbed over a neighbor's fence to turn off a hose that they had left running before leaving for a vacation. The entire back porch was flooded. I had to climb their fence because it was locked. After doing my "good deed" of turning off the water, I had to climb the fence again to get out of their backyard. My shoes were wet and as I landed, one of my toes dislocated. It was excruciating pain! I had never experienced a dislocation, so I was afraid to let anyone touch my toe. When I finally allowed a doctor to pull my toe out of its dislocation and return it into its proper position, I was surprised at how quickly the pain went away.

I was learning to trust God completely, and I was learning to cooperate with whatever He was bringing me through. I had accepted that parts of this journey called life include pain. But I also wanted to believe that someday I could say with confidence, "Whom the Lord sets free is free indeed!"

JOURNAL ENTRY: 12/5/16

I got my infected tooth pulled out today by an oral surgeon. It was one of my back molars, and it had been infected for a long time. It was starting to affect my health, and the dentist told me I had no choice but to have it pulled. I was so scared. I didn't want to lose my molar. I was afraid of the pain and honestly, I didn't want to part with my tooth. Even though it was dead and infected, it was my tooth. It was a part of me, and it had been in my mouth for many years. I really didn't want to let it go.

The surgeon, Dr. MacKenzie, was very kind and gentle. He gave me some laughing gas, which helped calm my nerves. As he began to pull the molar, I heard some cracking noises. The tooth crumbled within his tools. He explained to me that he had removed the tooth, but he would also have to remove the roots because they were also infected. He told me that the roots were three-pronged and very deep, so he would have to use some tools to break them apart. My jaw was numbed with Novocain, so I felt no pain, but when he told me that the roots were deep and three-pronged, I could feel tears starting to run down my cheeks.

I held still, of course. Now that I was committed, I wanted all three parts of the root removed. Dr. MacKenzie gently explained each part of the process as he tapped the base of the root to break it apart. As I laid there in surgery, my thoughts went to my wedding day with Frank. They had mentioned a scripture that day which said, "A three-stranded cord is not easily broken," which meant that if a married couple included God in their union, it would not be easily broken.

As I lay there with my eyes closed, I imagined Dr. MacKenzie as God the surgeon. I don't know how or why my marriage got infected, but it did. And God pulled me out of it. As I lay there listening to the tapping and feeling the tugging as he pulled each part of the root out, I surrendered in my mind to let it go. I also surrendered to God to let my broken marriage go.

After Dr. MacKenzie left the room, his assistant came in and asked me how I was doing. There were tears streaming down my face, so she asked me if I was okay. I said, "Was the doctor able to get all three parts of the root out?" She said yes. She rubbed my back and gave me instructions for the healing.

Then she said, "Just a minute, I have something for you." When she came back into the room, she handed me a small container of vanilla ice cream with a plastic spoon. She said, "The cold of the ice cream will help with the healing."

Now, to finish healing physically, emotionally, and spiritually. I want to become healthy. I want to allow myself to be "free indeed!"

34

Freedom!

I was surprised when Rebecca asked me to help out with another women's meeting at the church. I didn't feel like I was ready to help anyone. I was still healing. Yet I wasn't too surprised, considering she had already encouraged me to volunteer in the church nursery and help lead a women's prayer group! She seemed to really believe that "whom the Lord sets free is free indeed." There's no time for groveling with this woman!

Meredith Page had been invited to come to our church for a special women's meeting on inner healing. I was very excited to attend because I had just finished reading her book *Journey of Survival*. She was a new role model for me because of her courage to trust in God's love despite having to go through a great deal of trauma.

We were given name badges to wear during the meeting.

We had gathered together at the church the night before so Rebecca could explain to us the outline of the meeting. She told us to prepare our hearts to be used by God and to pray for the speaker as well as the women who would come.

I was unsure as I walked into church that night. I didn't really want to be used by God; I just wanted to be healed. As soon as Meredith began to speak, I felt like God's presence was in the room. The sanctuary was packed with over 100 women. My heart softened as I looked around the room. Maybe I wasn't the only one there feeling fragile.

Meredith told us that the enemy wants to imprison us in a dungeon with a lie. She said that the devil will feed us a lie, and that lie can trap us. She said sometimes we don't even realize it's a lie. Sometimes we believe the lie and sometimes, even when we know it's a lie, we still hold onto it in our minds.

She told us we need to ask the Holy Spirit to reveal the lie and when He does, we need to offer the lie to God and ask Him to take the lie away and replace it with a truth. This is easier said than done. I'm sure many of us have held onto lies about ourselves for years. At this point of the meeting, Meredith asked us to bow our heads and quietly ask the Holy Spirit to reveal any lie that the enemy may have us trapped in. I felt a rush of emotion and began to cry quite heavily. I hadn't even started to pray yet.

I knew the Holy Spirit wanted to show me a lie, so I calmed down and quieted my mind. I leaned forward in my chair and rested my head in my hands. My eyes were closed, and I prayed. I said, "Dear Heavenly Father, is there a lie I've been trapped in that you would like to reveal to me?" The lie came to me instantly: "God might someday fall out of love with you." I felt embarrassed. I thought I had already dealt with this lie. I had been struggling with this lie since I was twelve years old. From the moment I heard my father explain to us why he could no longer be married to my mother, I knew it was a lie. The words my father said that night were, "Someday you will understand that people can fall out of love."

Hadn't I dealt with this lie over and over again? Maybe Meredith was right. She had just told us that "sometimes, even when we know it's a lie, we still hold onto it in our minds." Maybe, as Meredith was suggesting, I had to actually hand the lie over to God in order to be completely freed from its grip.

I was still leaning forward in my chair with my head bowed. The lights had been turned low in the sanctuary, and I could hear the quiet hum of women praying. I realized that I was still trapped in this lie, and God was offering me freedom from it.

I took a deep breath and thought to myself, *Okay, what am I supposed to do with this lie now? I'm supposed to ask God if He would please take the lie from me and replace it with a truth. I have to let go of the lie? I have to actually hand it over to God?*

You would think it would be easy, but it wasn't. I started crying again. I thought, *Well, I'll just give it a try.* I closed my eyes and prayed, "Dear Heavenly Father, the enemy has told me a lie. The lie is that you will someday fall out of love with me. Would you please take this lie and give me a truth in exchange?" Immediately a scripture verse came to my mind. It was the same passage of scripture that I had written in Charlie's baby book:

> *"Can a mother forget the baby at her breast and have no compassion on the child she has borne? Though she may forget, I will not forget you! See, I have engraved you on the palms of my hands; your walls are ever before me."*
> —*Isaiah 49:15,16*

I sat there crying softly. I was not the only person in the room crying. The Spirit of God was touching so many lives. Then I sat up and smiled. I looked around the room and felt God's love. What freedom! How beautiful it feels to let go of a lie and replace it with a truth! God loves me. He always has and He always will. He cannot and will not ever fall out of love with me! I felt amazing.

Meredith Page gave us all a wonderful tool to use for the rest of our lives: freedom from bondage. I tucked this strategy away for future use. "Whom the Lord sets free IS free indeed!"

35

The Party

I wonder if I will always recognize domestic abuse now. I had learned a lot in Cindy's Tuesday night classes. She taught us how to recognize the red flags of domestic abuse. It seems that although we all like to believe our relationships are unique, I learned in her class that an abuser's behavior patterns are very common and consistent. They all lie. They all blame someone or something else for their failures. They usually have a mother who supports and defends and excuses their behavior, and the list goes on. Most abusers are so good at their craft of confusion, control, and isolation that the victim doesn't even realize they are a victim.

Cindy's classes were a blessing to me. The information was difficult to take in, but what she was providing for us was freedom, if we wanted it. She taught with wisdom, humor, and love. Her class was a safe place where she could turn on a light and hold up a mirror, exposing the trap of abuse.

Now that I am free, how will I handle it when I recognize that someone is in an abusive relationship? I hope to handle it with wisdom, strength, and grace like Cindy does.

Tonight at our company Christmas party, I witnessed Sharon's boyfriend "act out" in the familiar way of abuse. We were having our party downtown at Alforno Trattoria. We had reserved a large table in the back room so we could all bring our spouses. When I got there, they had been just having drinks at the bar with a few appetizers. I came by myself and just wandered to each of my coworkers, greeting them and their husbands.

I noticed Sharon's boyfriend right away because he was acting weird in the familiar way that Frank did. He was fidgety and kept leaving the room to go outside. Also, his eyes looked weird. His pupils were totally dilated so that his eyes looked black. I saw the fear and embarrassment in Sharon's face. This was all too familiar to me. He was acting exactly like Frank did so many times. I felt my adrenaline go up, but I was not afraid.

A few minutes after we all sat down to eat, Sharon's boyfriend had an angry outburst and jumped up from his chair, knocking a few glasses off the table. He was yelling about something and acting like he wanted to punch the wall. We all just sat there staring at him, bewildered. Sharon was just looking down like she had seen this before, and she was embarrassed.

A husband of one of my friends told him to leave so he went outside, but we could hear him yelling and cussing from inside the restaurant. Allesia was about to call the police, but she didn't have to because the boyfriend finally left.

After that, we continued with our dinner and the Christmas party, trying our best to not make a big deal about it, but I was watching Sharon. Her daughters showed up after the gift exchange. I overheard Sharon's daughter ask Sharon if she wanted to spend the night at her house. Sharon said yes.

At least I know she will be safe tonight. How heartbreaking. On Monday I will talk with Sharon and encourage her to attend Cindy's classes with me. This makes me angry, and it breaks my heart.

36

Regret

As I entered into the holiday season, I was pleasantly surprised by my lack of anxiety. Christmastime had always been challenging for me emotionally, but not this year. I not only survived the holidays, I thrived!

I was happy and content as I prepared to travel to Greenville for our family Christmas party. This was a new feeling for me, since traveling with Frank over the last few years had become very hard. In the early years of our marriage, I didn't really notice that Frank had a "pattern of abuse." He seemed to be very lovable and happy most of the time. He had a goofy, boyish quality about him that was fun. My family loved and embraced him and, in the early years, holiday visits were great! Frank, Charlie, and I spent many weekends at my dad and Abby's house. Those weekends were carefree, relaxed, and casual. The holidays with my family in Greenville were pleasant in the early years.

But it didn't take long for that to change. It was subtle at first. So subtle that I didn't recognize it as a pattern until I was ready to leave him. But looking back, I could see that his behavior was very consistent and strange to me. Everything would be seemingly normal and happy in our home until something would trigger Frank to get angry.

The first time I noticed it was a month into our marriage. I had picked up our mail and brought it up to our new apartment. There were a few ads, some wedding cards, and our first power bill. I left the mail on the counter to look through with Frank when he came home from work. Charlie was doing his homework in the living room, and I was making dinner when Frank came home. I walked over to him and gave him a kiss and a hug and said, "Look, Frank, our first mail!"

He picked it up and sorted through the envelopes, then opened up the power bill. His eyes glanced down the page, and then he threw the open bill onto the countertop and said, "Are you kidding me? That's way too expensive! I'm not paying that!" Then he proceeded to cuss and grumble on his way to the bedroom. I followed him and tried to talk with him about how we were going to handle the bills, but he was angry. He was yelling at me as he took off his boots, noisily throwing each one towards the closet.

This made me feel very uncomfortable. I didn't like this type of behavior, and I wasn't used to it. Charlie and I were used to a peaceful, loving home. I knew Charlie was in the living room and that he was probably more uncomfortable than I was. I confronted Frank and told him to calm down, the first of many times I would let him know his behavior was unacceptable to me. Then he stormed out of the apartment to "cool down."

Over the next eleven years, this pattern of behavior continued. Sometimes months would go by, but then the pattern would rear its ugly head. Something would trigger Frank's temper, and he would act out, either by cussing and throwing things or by withdrawing completely and sleeping for hours or days.

The last year, leading up to me walking out, was the worst. And that is when I started to hear the Lord calling my name. That was when the Lord led me to Cindy Sprague's classes on domestic abuse. That was when my eyes opened up to typical patterns of abuse, which Frank had. And that was when I started to find evidence of drug use. And finally, that was when I discovered that Frank was having an affair.

Like many domestic abuse survivors, physical or emotional, I have grappled with regret. They say that "hindsight is 20/20," and I now believe that to be true. Looking back, I can see clearly that I was trapped in a very abusive pattern. Trapped by my wishful thinking that I could somehow help Frank to handle his problems with anger and life and trapped by believing that Frank would someday change.

But do I have regret? No. I don't have time or energy for regret. I believe God allowed me to marry Frank, and

I believe it was God who pulled me out of the marriage. If God is who He says He is, then I have no choice but to believe the Bible when it says that "in all things God works for the good of those who love Him, who have been called according to His purpose" (Romans 8:28). I choose to look forward with hope rather than to look back with regret.

37

Moving Forward

It seems strange to me that everyone has to eat food to stay alive. I don't like to eat. Sometimes I'm afraid that food will make me feel sick, like it did when I first left Frank. Also, it's lonely to eat by myself. Lately, I've been watching people as they eat. There seems to be a common pattern. People usually sit down to eat. They pause from whatever they are busy with and consume their food. And people seem to like to have their meal with company.

My last client today was Sue Spencer and while her color was processing, we talked about what we were planning to have for dinner. Neither of us had any plans, and we were both hungry. She told me her husband Rob was on his way to the salon to pick her up, and he had asked her if she would like for him to bring her something to eat. She said, "I just want some soup. Would you like for him to bring enough for you?"

I said, "Sure! I'm starving and I would love to have some soup with you!"

The three of us sat around the table in the breakroom and enjoyed a bowl of hot soup together. It was minestrone, and it was delicious! As we ate, we talked about the day's events and laughed and just enjoyed eating together. It was pleasant, and I will never forget how much it meant to me. Rob and Sue know I've been going through a tough time emotionally, and they seem to go out of their way to just show me God's love.

When I feel better, I want to remember to be aware of people who live alone. I want to look for opportunities to share my meal with someone who is going through a hard time. I've now had the privilege of experiencing how this type of sharing God's love feels.

The holiday season this year was surprisingly fun! I enjoyed every little thing about it. I took the time to appreciate my family, my friends, my coworkers, and my clients. I did not spend time looking back and feeling sorry for my losses. I was doing my best to trust God with my past, my present, and my future. And I was trusting that God was healing my broken heart. I filled my days with structure and chose joy. It helped me emotionally to sleep when it was time to sleep, eat when it was time to eat, and work when it was time to work. I also started to include new activities into my routine. I joined a tap dance class that met every Friday afternoon. It felt refreshing to try something new. I wasn't a very good student but I noticed myself smiling and laughing a lot. It's hard to feel sad when you are hopping around in a dance studio, listening to the clicking and clacking of your own tap shoes!

Things were starting to settle into a new norm. I went through spring, summer, and fall in my new apartment, and now it was winter. It had been eight months since I left Frank and two months since I divorced him. Now to move forward. I knew God was healing my heart, and I accepted that some days would be harder than others, so I just kept to my new healthy structure and trusted God would guide me.

One day as I was putting away my clean laundry, I noticed my guitar case propped up in the back of my closet. My brother Jared gave it to me several years earlier. He is a musician, and I always enjoyed listening to him play guitar. In my twenties, I learned how to play a few chords and sang a song but never went any further. Jared heard me play and, years later, he gave me one of his guitars, encouraging me to continue. I remembered when he gave it to me. Jared and his family were visiting us at our house up here in Madison. I asked Jared to draw me a picture of the strings so I could know where to place my fingers to play one of my favorite U2 songs, "Running to Stand Still." I remember being excited to receive my first guitar, and I felt honored that my brother gave it to me, but I didn't see myself as a musician. Still, I learned to play that song. I remember playing it in our house. Frank and Charlie were busy doing other things, and I was sitting in the living room, strumming the chords and quietly singing. I was playing poorly, and it sounded horrible, but I was enjoying it, and I remember that my dog Lady was laying by my feet. It seemed to me that she was enjoying my music too.

JOURNAL ENTRY: 12/28/16

I've taken my guitar out of its case, and I've been teaching myself how to play chords. It's been four years since I've taken it out of its case. I feel a small portion of what my dear brother must have felt in his youth. We had to endure and heal from the trauma of abandonment from our father.

I remember a few years after my dad left that my brother got an electric guitar. He taught himself how to play it. Every day after school, my brother would finish his homework quickly so he could spend time playing his guitar. I would spend the afternoons sitting in his room with him, just listening to him as he learned new songs. The music that came from his hands on that guitar soothed my innermost being. I would often prop myself on his bed with a view of the setting sun, watching his fingers play the guitar. The music touched my soul. Sometimes I would fall to sleep as he played. I will never forget those days. They felt magical.

Now here I am, eagerly pushing through my workday so I can get home to my guitar, the acoustic guitar Jared gave me! It feels special. My fingers hurt and the chords don't sound very good, but still it soothes me. I feel comforted. I miss my brother!!

38

The Word

My Catholic angel Gabby told me at work today that the Lord will give me a "word" for 2017. She said that last year her word was "hope." She said, "The Holy Spirit will speak the word to you, and that word will try you and you will learn to embrace that word in your life. You might hear the word in passing or see the same word written repeatedly."

I didn't really want to get a word for 2017. I'm still trying to process all the difficulties of 2016! I told her I would be open to receiving a "word" from the Holy Spirit but that I really didn't . . . and before I could finish my sentence a word came to my mind. The word was "passion." I didn't tell her.

I don't think that will be my word since I've just been through a divorce and I've taken back my maiden name. Maybe it will be a passion for serving God? Anyway, since I'm keeping a journal, I figured I'd make a note of it.

I was happy that 2016 was coming to a close. I know it's just a date on the calendar, but I was ready for a new year. I had no idea what the Lord had in store for me, but I had learned to trust Him completely. There's a verse in the Bible that says, "The heart of a man plans his way, but the LORD establishes his steps" (Proverbs 16:9, ESV).

After the divorce was final, I had considered moving back to Greenville to be closer to my family. But then I thought to myself, *If I leave Madison now and go back to Greenville, I will leave with bad feelings towards Madison.* That didn't seem fair. What did the city of Madison ever do to me? It was tempting to move away and leave all the painful memories behind me, but what about the good memories? I didn't want to do anything out of fear or pain, so I decided to just stay put.

39

The Violin Lesson

JOURNAL ENTRY: 1/1/17

"Trust in the Lord with all your heart and lean not on your own understanding. In all your ways acknowledge Him and He will direct your paths." —Proverbs 3:5,6

What's my secret? Total surrender, total trust, total obedience. It's a discipline and it's hard, but it's easier when you surrender to God's leading. His yoke isn't hard unless you're fighting against it. God is for you; He's not against you. The enemy is against you. You might even be against yourself, But God is for you. Let go.

It was the first morning of a new year, and I was feeling happy and content. The house was quiet, and the sun was pouring some long-awaited sunshine into my little bedroom. I made myself a cup of instant coffee and crawled back into my bed. I situated the pillows behind my back so I could sit up and look out the window. The sky was a clear deep blue. Even though the sun was shining brightly, I knew it was cold outside. It was still winter. My beloved trees stood tall and proud, even though they had been stripped of their leaves. Their branches looked like skinny twigs reaching to the sky. There they stood, lined up neatly in a row, patiently waiting for spring.

Charlie was gone for the weekend, and I was all caught up on errands, so the day was open to do whatever I wanted to do. I started the day like every other day, enjoying a cup of coffee with the Lord. I loved to open the Bible and read scriptures. I would read and imagine those words were written for me specifically, as if the Lord loved me so much that He wanted to write a story about it. Sometimes I felt a sense of deep comfort, like the Lord Himself was right there next to me, reading over my shoulder.

The morning sun was still pouring into my room as I finished my cup of coffee. I was very much enjoying the fact that today was a day off and there was no need to rush. After a little while, I got up and made my bed. I wandered around the apartment, enjoying the fact that everything was clean and tidy. *Now what to do?*

I walked back into my bedroom and picked up my

guitar. I had been practicing every day, trying to learn the chords to U2's song, "Wild Horses." It was pretty hard to play. The strings hurt my fingers but if I didn't press down hard enough, the guitar didn't sound good. I was finally able to play every chord except for the F chord. That one was weird, so I just played through the song without the F. It sounded good enough for me to sing along with in my own company. I was having fun!

After a short while I started to get bored. It was New Year's Day and everything was closed. All my friends were busy with family, and my family was far away. I glanced across the room and saw the new violin that Jared and Amélie had given to me for Christmas. I had told them I came across my old violin when I moved everything from storage into my new apartment. I had asked them if they knew of anyone who could fix it up for me so I could teach myself how to play again. Instead, they surprised me with a beautiful new violin for Christmas!

I wanted to pick it up and try to play it, but I had been advised against teaching myself this instrument. It was my client Stan who had suggested that I get proper training. I had told him that I was teaching myself to play the guitar and that I just got a new violin and I was going to teach myself how to play that too.

"Oh no . . . you don't want to try to teach yourself how to play the violin. You can teach yourself how to play the guitar, but with the violin, you need to learn proper mechanics or you might develop a poor technique that will be difficult to unlearn." He told me that his daughter Sean played the violin very well, and she was going to be home from college for the holidays. He said she would probably be more than happy to give me a basic beginners lesson.

Just then I remembered I had told Stan I would love to take him up on his offer and that New Year's Day might work for me! I couldn't believe I had forgotten all about it! Maybe it was because I had been so busy during the holidays. Or maybe it was because I was a little apprehensive about meeting up with a client at his home. Either way, I had suddenly remembered we'd made a tentative plan for me to go to his place for a casual violin lesson with his daughter sometime after breakfast on New Year's Day.

Oh boy! I glanced at the little alarm clock on my desk. It was just past 10:00 a.m. so I wasn't going to be too late. I looked across my sun-filled room at the violin propped against the corner. I really wanted to try to play it, but I agreed with Stan's advice. I gathered up my courage and dialed Stan's phone number.

"Hello?" said Stan with his deep voice.

"Oh, hi, Stan. This is Rose," I said nervously. "Is today still a good day for me to come over for a violin lesson with your daughter?"

"Yes, it is," said Stan. "She told me that today would work out perfectly for her. She's excited to meet you!"

"Um . . . okay! What time should I come over?" I said, feeling a little awkward.

"Anytime," said Stan. "Sean and Jude told me they would be here around eleven."

"Great!" I said. "Text me your address, and I'll head over to your place."

"Okay!" he said nicely. "See you soon."

After I hung up, I quickly put on a decent-looking outfit, grabbed my violin, and headed out the door. What a beautiful day! I was so happy I was going out to do something fun. It took a little bit of courage, but not much. I did not want to end up becoming someone who stayed locked in a cage of fear and sorrow forever. Yes, what I went through in the previous nine months was very hard emotionally. But God had been with me even in the scariest and darkest moments. Why couldn't I trust Him to be with me in the healing? I was feeling better every day. God was healing my broken heart, and I had no time for fear.

I was shocked to find out that Stan lived literally four minutes away from my apartment. I felt very happy and peaceful as I drove over to his place. I wasn't afraid. In fact, I had the strange feeling that God was orchestrating this meeting.

I will never forget the moment when I walked into Stan's house for the first time. I knocked on the front door and heard Stan say, "Come in!" I opened the door and, as I walked in, I said, "It smells good in here." Stan greeted me and asked if I would like a cup of coffee. "Sure!" I said. It would be a pleasant change from my boring instant coffee.

I set my violin down on the sofa and walked over to the dining room table. I sat down and waited for Stan to pour me a cup of coffee. I felt embarrassed for saying, "It smells good in here." I was surprised I even said it out loud. The truth was that it smelled familiar. It was more of a feeling than a smell. It felt like family, like safety. It felt like a real home.

The two of us sat together at the dining room table, waiting for Sean and Jude to show up. We were both very comfortable. I was glad I wasn't feeling awkward. At one point I stood up and walked into the kitchen and asked if I could pour myself a glass of water. "Sure!" Stan said. "The glasses are in the cupboard above the dishwasher." I helped myself to a glass and filled it up with water from the faucet. There was an opening in the wall between the kitchen and the dining room, so I just stood there drinking my water while Stan continued to chat with me.

As I stood there listening, I glanced down at the kitchen counter to my left. I noticed a small plate with a half-eaten muffin on it. I was starving! I realized I hadn't eaten any breakfast. *Oh man, I'm hungry,* I thought to myself. *What if I start feeling weak and get nervous before the violin lesson?* Without hesitation I asked Stan, "Is this your muffin?"

"Yes, I didn't finish eating it this morning."

"Oh," I said. "Can I eat the rest of it?"

"Sure."

So I just stood there, happily eating the other half of Stan's breakfast while he continued to chat with me. *How strange . . . why am I so comfortable here?* I thought to myself. *It must be because Stan is a Christian and God is with me, giving me peace.*

Just then the front door flew open, and in bounded

Stan's daughter Sean followed by her boyfriend Jude. They were smiling and laughing about something they had been discussing on their way in. *What a fun couple of kids*, I thought. They were about Charlie's age. I liked them immediately. Sean walked into the kitchen and made herself a hot cup of tea while Stan poured some coffee for Jude. We all sat around the table, talking and laughing for quite some time. I kept glancing at Sean. She was so beautiful. She was sitting to the left of me, and I was watching her laugh and smile as she chatted with her dad. At one point I said to her, "Your face is so beautiful. It's clear to me that you must resemble your mother!"

She turned to me and smiled and said, "Thank you," while the others laughed at my attempt to make fun of Stan.

After that, Sean and I went into the living room, and she took my violin and played a beautiful song for me. She told me I had a very nice instrument with good tonal quality. I was very impressed with how casual she seemed. She was a professional level violinist but I didn't feel nervous about learning from her. She was a natural teacher, and I quickly learned how to hold the violin correctly and even where my fingers should go. I vaguely remembered playing as a child but after her lesson, I felt it would come back to me. She complimented me and said I had a good ear for music. That meant a lot to me, coming from a real musician.

A few hours went by comfortably, and I enjoyed every minute of my visit. Eventually Sean and Jude said they needed to leave because they were planning to spend the afternoon with Jude's parents. I felt like it would be a good time for me to leave too, so we all walked out to our cars together. I hugged Sean and thanked her for the lesson and told her I was so happy to meet her. I hugged Jude too. I really liked him and enjoyed talking about mathematics and physics with him. He was a very smart and kind young man, and I liked him right away. Then I turned to Stan and said, "Thank you so much for encouraging me to come over for a violin lesson. I had so much fun and I really love your family!" Then without thinking twice, I reached out and gave him the biggest hug.

He smiled and said, "I'm glad you came over. It was really fun!"

As I drove away from Stan's house, I turned right instead of left. I wasn't quite ready to go back to my apartment. I was overcome with emotion, and I didn't know why. I didn't know where to go or what to think, so I just drove. As I drove, I felt like I needed to go to the river. There is a beautiful river that runs through our valley, and I have spent a lot of time near it. I knew of a place not too far from my apartment where Frank and I used to go when I wanted to fly-fish. So I drove to that spot.

As I pulled into the place where we used to park, I realized that today was still New Year's Day and nobody was there. The parking lot was empty. I felt a little insecure and realized I had never been to the river alone. I parked as close as I could to the pathway. I knew it well but had never been there by myself. I was a little hesitant about getting out of my car, but I felt like I needed to stand by the river. I wanted to pray.

I gathered my courage and stepped out of the car and walked up to the riverbank. Ahh, there was the river in all its beauty! Rough and dangerous yet beautiful and full of life. The sun was still shining brightly, which made the water all the more welcoming to gaze upon. I stood there quietly, listening to the sound of the water. Then the tears began to roll down my cheeks. *Why am I crying? I just had the most amazing visit with a beautiful family!* Still, the tears came. It wasn't because I was missing Frank or thinking about former times fishing there. The river seemed different. The sky and the sun seemed different. The air smelled different. It seemed new, healthy, and right. I knew I had to pray.

"Dear Lord," I said out loud, "thank you for this beautiful day. Thank you for the amazing visit I just had with Stan and his family. Thank you for always being with me and for healing my broken heart. Thank you for everything you have done. Thank you for everything you are doing and thank you for everything you are planning to do. I trust you."

As I finished praying, I realized I was standing next to a river in a pretty desolate place, completely alone. I'm a woman, and I know better than to put myself in a vulnerable position. The water was glistening so beautifully in the sunshine that I wanted to linger, but the place was quiet and surrounded by shrubs and bushes where any predator could be hiding. I felt a tinge of fear. If someone were to come out of hiding to attack me, I was without protection.

I decided it was best to leave the river and go home. I turned away from the river and started walking up the dirt path towards my car. I didn't want to be afraid, but I was suddenly aware that being alone in a place like that wasn't the wisest choice. When I made it to the parking lot, I could see my car in the distance. It was the only car in the lot. *Why was it taking so long to get to my car?* I thought. The large bushes and shrubs that lined the river also lined the parking lot. *I hope no one jumps out of those bushes to attack me!*

I was annoyed by my own fear. I think I was also annoyed by the realization that I was really alone. For the first time in a long time, I was a single woman. And at this particular moment, it didn't feel so wonderful. The car seemed forever away, but I just kept walking. I wished that Charlie or one of my friends were with me. I wished that Stan were with me. I didn't feel safe by myself. I felt pressured to say another prayer as I walked. It came out honestly.

"Dear Lord, I just want you to know that I am very happy being single, but if you think that it would be better for me to married again someday, I trust you." Finally, I arrived at the car. I got inside, locked the doors, and drove away. I felt happy. The sun was still shining, and it was a beautiful afternoon. I was excited to get back to my apartment. It was a new year, and God was healing my broken heart. It felt refreshing to trust God. I felt a hope that God had good plans for me.

Church Date

B y the middle of the following week, I noticed I had been thinking a lot about Stan and his family. So Wednesday night I decided to give Stan a call. I had such a beautiful visit on New Year's Day, and I wanted to thank him again. I didn't let myself get nervous or overthink the situation; I just picked up my phone and dialed his number.

"Hello?" said Stan in his recognizable deep voice.

"Oh, hi Stan, this is Rose," I said, with a smile on my face.

"Hi Rose," Stan said. "How are you doing?"

"I'm doing great!" I said. "I've been thinking all week about our New Year's Day visit and how much fun I had, and I just wanted to thank you again for inviting me over."

Stan told me that he really enjoyed it too and that Sean and Jude also had a great time.

I felt very comfortable talking with Stan. I didn't know him personally, but he had been my client for several years so talking with each other came easily. Calling a client for anything other than work was different though, but Stan made me feel very safe and comfortable.

We chatted for a little while and then he asked, "Do you go to that church downtown?"

"Yeah," I answered, "I go to Green Valley Church."

"I thought so," he said. "I have a few friends from my church that attend Green Valley now, and I've been wanting to visit one of their services."

"Oh," I said. "If you ever want to go to a Saturday night service, send me a text and I'll meet you at the door. We can sit together. I go every Saturday night."

"Sounds great!" Stan said. "What time does the service start?"

"Six o'clock," I said.

Saturday afternoon I received a text from Stan. He was wondering if he could meet me at church that evening. I sent a text back saying, "Sure! Wait for me in the lobby. I should be just a couple minutes late; I'm coming straight from work." We sat together and listened to the sermon. It felt strange sitting next to someone in church since I had been attending alone for the past nine months, but it also felt nice.

When the service was over, I asked Stan if he would walk upstairs to the nursery with me. I had been volunteering once a month to help with the babies, and I had noticed a small guitar hanging on the wall with broken strings. I thought it would be nice to play a few chords for the children once in a while, but I didn't know how to restring a guitar. Stan was willing to check it out. He loves guitars!

On our way up to the nursery we were stopped by Pastor Tim. He said hi to me and introduced himself to Stan. I thought that maybe Pastor Tim was feeling protective over me. I had gotten fairly close to Pastor Tim and Rebecca over the last year. It seemed like the two men were happy to meet each other. They both stood, eye to eye, shaking hands when I heard Pastor Tim ask, "Do you play bass guitar?"

"Yes, I do," said Stan, still shaking Pastor Tim's hand.

"Oh good," Pastor Tim said to Stan, "We need a bass player in our worship band."

The evening was beginning to feel a little surreal, but I felt happy and healthy. As we both began to walk toward the exit, I realized I was very, very hungry! Saturdays are busy at work for me, and I usually just make it to church with no time to eat until after the meeting. As we walked together toward the door, I was hoping Stan would ask me out for dinner. If he didn't, that was okay too. I would just eat something at home. Either way, I was going to ask Stan to walk me to my car. I usually had one of the ushers walk me to my car after service, but tonight I had Stan.

We opened the church doors to leave and were blasted with freezing cold air. It was still January. The pavement looked slick, and there was still snow on the edges of the road. This was a particularly cold winter.

"Would you walk me to my car?" I asked Stan.

"Of course," he replied. "Where are you parked?"

"Over there, about a block away," I said as I pointed down the street.

We took one step out the door, and Stan lost his footing and slipped on the ice. It was slick. I stood there watching him struggle to stand up and said, "Oh! I'm so sorry! Are you okay?!" The street was very black and shiny. You could see from the reflection of the street lights that it was icy.

"Yes, I'm okay," Stan said as he struggled to stand upright. We took one more step, and his right foot slipped on the street like he was on an ice-skating rink, throwing his leg into the air and flipping his body onto the cold asphalt once again. I couldn't believe it! I glanced down at the bottom of his shoe as he struggled to get up again, and I could see from the glow of the streetlight that the soles of his shoes were smooth. I started to laugh out loud. He glanced up at me and I said, "I'm sorry! I can't help you! You're too big for me to try to help up, and it's too icy for me to move!" I kept laughing while he struggled to stand up. Tears were starting to roll down my face.

"I'm so sorry for laughing!" I said. "I don't usually laugh when people fall or trip, and I don't know why I'm laughing now. What type of shoes are you wearing?!"

Stan finally got himself situated and able to stand upright. We both stood there for a moment, and I put my arm in his. "I'm wearing dress shoes."

And I started laughing even harder. "Wait, don't move,"

I said. "Where are you parked?" Stan pointed to his car that was parked along the curb about ten steps from where we were standing. "Can you just drive me to my car?" I asked.

"That's a great idea," said Stan. When we got into Stan's car, he asked me if I had eaten dinner yet.

"No," I said, "and I'm starving!"

"Why don't we go out for dinner, and then I'll bring you back to your car? My treat."

JOURNAL ENTRY: 1/7/17

Met with Stan at church tonight. We sat together during the service and then went to the nursery to pick up the little guitar I had asked him to fix. I asked him to walk me to my car, but he slipped on the ice and fell. Then I asked him to drive me to my car, which he did, but on the way he asked me if I'd eaten yet and I said no. He took me to Peppino's, and we had spaghetti and meatballs for dinner. We stayed and talked until the restaurant closed at 9:30 p.m.! It was sweet and honest and fun. So healthy. I cried on the way home because I felt overwhelmed. Not afraid. I can be healthy, and I can trust my God.

Highlights from the date:

Stan told me that his mother had a particularly dry sense of humor. He told me a funny story about how one time, when he was talking with his mom, he was telling her about how his job was going. He mentioned to her that it seemed like lately, the only people who constantly needed his help at work were the single middle-aged women, to which she replied, as if feeling compassion for the women, "They must be desperate." I thought it was funny.

While we were driving back to my car, I told Stan I thought that Pastor Tim probably came over to introduce himself because he was worried that I might be dating. Then I said out loud, "Gross!" And then Stan said, "Gross? Gee thanks." And then I said, "Not you . . . just dating." He smiled as if he understood what I meant. When I got out of his car, I looked back and said, "Am I reminding you of your mom?" He said, "Yes."

41

Redemption

The year 2017 was showing promise of becoming a good one. I was glad to be done with 2016. As I looked back through my journal, I was reminded of how difficult that year had been for me. But was it fair to allow a year to be horrible? I'm sure many good things also happened in 2016. People got married, people had babies, people graduated from college, people started new careers. The list could go on. Just because something terrible happened to me in 2016 didn't mean that it was a terrible year.

The year 2016 was also when I heard the Lord call me closer to Himself. It was the year I completely surrendered to God and showed it outwardly by being publicly baptized. It was in 2016 that I got to watch God open up impossible doors for me to get out of an abusive home and into a safe place. As hard and scary as it was, it was also amazing to see

God open up a way for me. I felt like one of the children of Israel walking through the middle of the Red Sea. In many ways, 2016 was an amazing year for me!

I don't think it's healthy to attach a negative emotion to a certain year or place or thing. When I was a child, I liked how fire looked when it came out of the gas burner on the stove top. I would stand there and stare at it. It was intriguing and beautiful. My mother was constantly telling me to stand back because the flame of the fire could hurt me. I did eventually put my finger into the flame to feel it, and it did hurt me. I learned that fire is dangerous to touch, so I never touched it again. But I did not become terrified of fire. I still like fire and use it often to cook or warm myself by a campfire or to simply enjoy the soft glow of candlelight. There is a difference between wisdom and fear.

My challenge now was to know the difference. I did not want to live in fear. It's too toxic and debilitating. If God was able to rescue me from abuse, then God was able to heal my emotions. I would be patient with the process. I was not going to live in a state of PTSD forever. I wanted to "see the goodness of God in the land of the living" (Psalm 27:13).

I started to experience what I call "redemption." To redeem something means to buy it back. At first, it wasn't intentional but out of necessity. When I moved into my new apartment, I was fortunate to have all of my household items available to me. Although I snuck out of my mother-in-law's house with just the clothes on my back and whatever I could fit into my car in fifteen minutes, I also had a key to our storage unit, which was full of the rest of our household supplies. This felt like both a blessing and a curse. It was a blessing because I could set up my new apartment without being a burden to anyone. The curse was that each item held a memory of my eleven years of marriage with Frank.

God was with me every moment as I set up the apartment. It was a time of grief and acceptance. At first, every single item brought back a memory. But out of necessity, I had to keep many of the items. There was the beautiful hand-crafted wood table and bench set that my brother had given to us for our first home in Madison. There were the cobalt blue dinner plates that my Aunt Connie had given to us as a wedding gift. And the list went on. I only kept what I needed, but I needed a lot to set up my new home. At first, it was difficult. The items brought back memories.

But I was patient with the process. It took time to go through each box from the storage unit. I had contacted Frank by text, and he told me he didn't want anything that was in storage. It took time to decide which items to keep, what to give away, and what to throw away. I allowed myself to acknowledge the memories each item brought to mind, and I would sometimes cry and sometimes smile and sometimes feel physically sick. By the time I had my apartment nicely set up, I had given away or sold more than half of my belongings. I also gave a large box full of Frank's personal items to my sister-in-law, Linda, to give back to Frank.

As I settled into my new apartment, I was still surrounded by items that reminded me of my marriage and life with Frank. I wondered if those feelings would last forever, but they didn't. Old memories began to be replaced by new memories. The beautiful wood dining room table, that had been in the center of my home with Frank, now had a new purpose. It was where Charlie and I had our first Thanksgiving dinner together, safe and happy. And it was the gathering place for Charlie and his friends on many summer evenings as they played games and talked and laughed together. As time went by and I allowed my emotions to heal, I was learning to acknowledge the pain, forgive myself and those who hurt me, and to be patient with the process of healing.

JOURNAL ENTRY: 1/13/17

"Weekend at Anderson's"

Went to Greenville for the weekend. This is my first time visiting the place where I drew a line in the sand regarding Frank's anger. My first time visiting their home since that horrible Thanksgiving Day over a year ago.

It is important to address the negative memories. Confront them, acknowledge them, walk into the places of past hurt and look at them. Cry, be angry, be sorry, forgive. Then accept, breathe, smile and move on.

Redeem that place. See it as it now is so that past hurts do not taint something that is beautiful.

42

Ups And Downs

When I agreed to keep a journal for a year, I had no idea what that year was going to be like. But I knew that God was involved in every detail of my experience, and I knew I had to share it with the world. God rescued me out of an impossible situation, and I wanted to write about it so others could be encouraged to trust Him.

Every person's story is unique, and God wants to be involved in every detail. Looking back through my journal, I can see that my year was filled with many highs and lows. Life can be like that. We all have wonderful experiences and horrible experiences. God wants to walk with us through each one.

I could not have imagined that within one year I would go from grief over lost love to joy over new love, but that's how it happened with me. The process isn't always easy, but it's easier when you allow yourself to really trust God.

When I returned home from my visit to Greenville, I was exhausted. It took courage to revisit the Anderson's home and confront the memories of that horrible Thanksgiving

> *The process isn't always easy, but it's easier when you allow yourself to really trust God.*

Day, but I was glad I did. I knew somehow that I was processing the trauma. I was acknowledging that something horrible had happened to me and that God had brought me through. I didn't need to stay sad or scared; I could move forward and trust God with my future.

I was happy to get back to my apartment and get back into my new routine, but I was tired. I grabbed a load of laundry and drove to the laundromat, and as I waited for my clothes to dry, I realized I was also hungry. As I waited, I started to feel depressed and lonely. My mind wandered back to my visit with the Andersons and how strange it was for me. I remembered walking up the driveway where I was greeted by Mark and Jo, running out to hug me. I had only a moment to remember that it was the same driveway Charlie had run down to chase Frank through the street in anger. Life goes on. Life had gone on for the Andersons, and life had gone on for me. I had to let the memories go.

JOURNAL ENTRY: 1/15/17

Exhaustion + hunger = not good. I'm standing outside at my car, grabbing my laundry to bring it into the apartment. I'm crying. I'm lonely. I see a car drive by. I am hoping that it is my abuser. My lost lover. I'm still broken. I will put my laundry away. Take a bath. Listen to Christian music and go to sleep. My true lover sees me. I trust Him to heal me.

JOURNAL ENTRY: 1/18/17

It's been seventy-eight days since I've had contact by text with Frank. It's been nine months since I've seen him and three months since we've been divorced. I want closure. I want to see him and apologize for my part and forgive and hug and wish him all the best.

Is he passive-aggressive? Angry? Hurt? Doesn't care? I don't know, but God does. I will leave it alone and wait. God knows my heart. I will leave it in God's hands and trust Him.

CHAPTER

Prism Pizza

The following weekend, I met with Stan at church again. I liked attending the Saturday night services, but I was always hungry because I had to rush over from work. After the service ended, Stan offered to take me out for a bite to eat, so I suggested we go to Prism Pizza. I knew Charlie was working, and I wanted to introduce him to Stan. When we got to the restaurant, I asked if we could have Charlie serve us.

After waiting for a bit, Charlie came walking towards us with a nice smile on his face. He said, "Hi mom!"

I smiled back and said, "Hi, Charlie, this is Stan!"

Charlie shook Stan's hand and said, "It's nice to meet you!"

Stan smiled at Charlie and said, "It's very nice to meet you!"

As Charlie walked us back to a table, he said, "It's not

very busy right now; you guys are welcome to stay as long as you want." That was sweet, and we took full advantage of his offer.

The restaurant was large but still comfortable. It was a family-friendly pizza place. The center area was filled with large picnic-style tables where families or large parties could eat together. Along the back walls were small cozy booths. The tables, walls, and booths were made with blonde knotty pine wood, and the entire place was decorated with brightly colored artwork. Each table had a different style of glass lantern hanging overhead, which gave the room a soft glow.

Stan and I enjoyed our meal and talked for hours. Charlie stopped by now and then to see how we were doing and to refill our drinks. The hours flew by effortlessly as we laughed and talked about a wide range of subjects. At one point, Stan was telling me about some events that had happened in his past. I sat there listening and interacting with him.

In the middle of his story, which was quite personal, he paused and said, "Wow! I don't know why I'm telling you all of this."

I replied, "It's because I'm your hairstylist!"

We laughed and laughed, and as I glanced across the room, I caught Charlie smiling at us.

JOURNAL ENTRY: 1/21/17

I had another dinner date with Stan tonight. We ate at Prism and had Charlie as our server.

Like last time, we both enjoyed each other's company and talked about everything—our lives, our hurts, our journey so far, and Jesus! It was another four-hour dinner!

I am including this in my story because I am committed to continue this journal for one full year. I would never have expected to date anyone ever again, let alone before my year was up, but here I am.

And I am not afraid. I have learned a little bit from Cindy's classes about what a healthy man looks like and that you want someone who loves Jesus more than anyone. I don't really want to be married, but a few pages back in this journal, I wrote that if God feels that it would be more efficient and better to finish my journey married, that I will. If not, I'm totally cool with going it alone.

I've surrendered my will to God's will. I died, I let go, I gave up. And I totally trust God. Plus, I've learned a little bit about boundaries. If I feel uncomfortable, I will just tell Stan. For now, this feels like a blessing and a healing time for both of us.

44

A Difficult Week

For some reason I have been very quiet at work and weepy every evening. I miss Frank. I am brokenhearted over our lost love, our lost marriage. I'm confused. I do not regret my decision; it's just that love hurts. And I feel it most when I'm tired. I need to be careful with my schedule now. It's getting full with work and fun things to do, but I need to allow time for rest, reflection, and healing.

I can see that my son is processing my divorce in his own way. Frank was in his life from ten years old to twenty-two. Charlie has a soft heart. He told me tonight that he is concerned for Stan. He said, "Mom, when you and Stan were eating at Prism the other night, I saw you both talking and laughing, and I saw Stan looking so happy. He seems innocent, and I don't want to see him get hurt."

This seemed sweet to me.

I don't want Stan hurt either. I don't want to hurt him or be hurt. I am still hurting in my heart over the loss of my husband Frank.

I want to run away and have everyone leave me alone. I'm thinking about moving to Mexico to help with a Christian orphanage for two years. I'll wait to see if God opens something up.

I am tired.

JOURNAL ENTRY: 1/24/17

I had the perfect weekend, other than thinking of Stan. I got all my errands done in a timely and happy manner. I went on a hike with Ellie and Tom and then had a lovely dinner and fellowship with them. I observed a happy, healthy couple. Peaceful, joyful, so nice. The few times my thoughts wandered towards Frank,

I was content to leave him in God's capable hands.

But then, why Stan? Why did God allow a widowed man to enter my life now? I'm not ready. I don't understand the ways of love, and I don't trust the institution of marriage or falling in love.

I don't want it.

I don't want to see Stan hurt. I don't want to be hurt. I'm not ready to trust.

JOURNAL ENTRY: 1/25/17

Today I finally saw a new post on Frank's Facebook page. It was a pic of him standing in front of some trees smiling. His girlfriend had taken the photo, and she captioned it, "My handsome man." He looked so happy.

I cried. Maybe he is happy now. Maybe people are attracted to me, but then at some point in time no longer want to be with me. Should I tell Stan to run for the hills?

This had been a difficult week for me. My emotions were all over the place. I stood up from my little desk and closed my journal. As I walked down the hall toward the bathroom to wash my face, I thought to myself, *It's one thing to feel sad, but to be afraid that everyone is going to fall out of love with you, or eventually stop liking you, doesn't seem healthy.*

I washed my face and remembered the women's church meeting I had gone to back in December. Maybe this was a lie that the enemy was trying to trap me in. I hurried back to my room and knelt at the edge of my bed to pray. I could do what Meredith Page had taught us to do whenever the enemy tries to trap us in a lie. I could give the lie to God and wait for Him to give me back a truth!

I did not realize at the time that the enemy was trying to trap me with a fear of abandonment. It was the same old lie, just wrapped differently.

I folded my hands together and closed my eyes. I had to give this lie to Jesus. I said out loud, "Dear Jesus, here is the lie that I think the devil has trapped me in. I feel that, although you might be attracted to me now, I'm afraid at some point you might want to get away from me. Please take this lie and give me a truth."

I opened my eyes and sat down on the floor to wait for Jesus to give me a truth. Immediately a Bible verse came to my mind: "Lo, I am with you. Even until the end of the world." What a quick answer! God was telling me He wanted to be with me. Even until the end of the world! I stood up and walked over to my nightstand. I picked up my phone and Googled the verse. It said:

"Go therefore and make disciples of all the nations,

baptizing them in the name of the Father and of the Son and of the Holy Spirit, teaching them to observe all things that I have commanded you; and lo, I am with you always, even to the end of the age. Amen" (Matthew 28:19, 20, NKJV).

I have been struggling with depression, crying, sadness, and fatigue all week.

I'm eating well, resting, exercising and reading the Bible. I feel so sad and so tired. I upped my vitamin D. Maybe it's just because it's winter?

Maybe I should tell Stan it's all too soon? Too soon for what?? He's not pressuring me in the least bit. He gives me full space. He is the sweetest blessing. He's a beautiful man, and I enjoy his company. I trust him, and I do not need to feel uncomfortable. If I need space and time, I've got it!

My sweet angel Gabby encouraged me at work today. She told me that I should pray and ask the Lord to cut any soul-ties I have with Frank. My spirit bears witness that this is good advice. I fell in love with Frank. I love him still. I hope that I will always love him. The Lord brought him to me, and I will always cherish the love we had. In those early days, I felt I had found my soulmate. I felt I had found the man God custom-made for me to join for all eternity. We even both have a rare "fingerprint" on our palms! It was something I had never seen before and likely will never see again. How could this perfect union break?

I remember my tooth pulling incident with my beloved Dr. MacKenzie. How sweetly and gently, but firmly, he broke the three-pronged root to remove the infected tooth. I remember how God woke me up and called to me and removed me from my union with Frank. I didn't understand it, and I didn't like it, but I surrendered to it.

Tonight, I will pray and ask God to cut the soul-tie I have with Frank. This is sad for me and painful, but I trust my God and my Creator. I can trust Him with all that concerns me.

JOURNAL ENTRY: 1/29/17

I'm struggling with a deep depression. I am so tired. I just want to sleep. When I go through the motions of being awake, it's as if I'm dreaming.

I went to church this morning and got to sit between Stan and Charlie! Although I was uncomfortable with being awake, it was a beautiful service and I felt blessed. Pastor Tim's opening prayer was enough for me. To it, I say amen! He prayed for deliverance from depression and addiction.

After church I had lunch with Stan at the Three Sisters Pub. It was good food, fun talk, and lots of laughter. I thank God for bringing Stan into my journey at this time. God brought him through his own journey of grief, and now he is a comfort to me.

"I believe that I shall look upon the goodness of the Lord in the land of the living! Wait for the Lord; be strong, and let your heart take courage; wait for the Lord!" —Psalm 27: 13,14

Switchfoot Concert

*"Behold, God is my salvation; I will trust,
and will not be afraid; for the Lord God is
my strength and my song, and He has become
my salvation."*

—Isaiah 12:2

Part of my new routine included listening to Christian music every night before drifting off to sleep. I would put on my earphones and listen to Klove radio through my phone app. Music comforted and inspired me. One night, while I was lying in bed, I heard a new song by Switchfoot called "Where the Light Shines Through." I felt like the lyrics were written just for me! I sat up in bed and turned on the light. I had to write a note to remind myself to buy the new album.

A few days later, I learned that the band was on tour and they would be playing a concert in a very small venue just thirty miles west of Madison! I was so excited that I bought two tickets for the show.

I thought that my date was going to be Charlie, but he already had plans to go on a ski trip with his friends. I didn't want to go to the concert by myself, but I really, really wanted to hear these new songs live! After work one evening, I sat at my desk, looking at my calendar. The concert was coming up in three days! *Maybe I should invite one of my friends to join me*? Then I thought about Stan. *Stan is a musician, and he would probably love to see Switchfoot live.* I had become very comfortable sitting with Stan at church, and I loved eating out with him after each service, but I wasn't too sure about going on a real date.

After musing about it for a while, I decided I should just call Stan. I couldn't stop thinking about him anyway, and I felt like this concert was going to be a healing time for me. I felt that Stan had compassion for what I was going through, and I realized I wanted to share this experience with him. I resisted the temptation to be afraid. I was done with fear. It wasn't going to be some kind of romantic date; we were just going to go to a Christian concert together!

I dialed Stan's number. "Hello?" Stan's voice put a smile on my face and butterflies in my stomach, which I didn't appreciate.

"Um, hi, Stan, this is Rose." I felt embarrassed.

"Hi, Rose. How are you doing?" said Stan. He didn't

sound nervous at all. I tried to ignore the butterflies in my stomach. There was nothing to be afraid of.

"Hey, I have two tickets to the Switchfoot concert this weekend, and I was wondering if you would like to go with me," I said confidently.

"Oh, wow! That sounds like fun! I'd love to!" Stan sounded happy.

"Sweet! It's this Sunday night at eight," I said. "Would you mind picking me up? It's a thirty-minute drive, so we might as well go together." Stan said that he would love to, and the date was set.

The next few days passed quickly and on Sunday evening, I looked out my bedroom window to see Stan's white truck pull into the apartment parking lot. I was ready to go so I grabbed my purse and keys and bounded down the staircase to meet Stan. I didn't even give him time to park his truck. He stopped in the middle of the parking lot when he saw me coming. He was smiling. I smiled back and opened the passenger door and hopped into his truck. The drive to the concert was enjoyable. We laughed and happily chatted about anything that came to mind.

When we arrived at the concert venue, I was happy to see that it was a small theater in the historic part of downtown. I love old buildings with their charming design and detailed woodwork. From the beveled walls to the spiral staircase, my eyes frantically searched to take it all in. The place was getting packed and there was an excitement in the air. Stan and I stood in the lobby as people of all ages hustled around us. Some were buying merchandise that was set up on the theater bar while others were rushing to the entrance doors which were on either side of lobby. It was open seating and Stan suggested that we look for a seat on the balcony. As we squeezed our way up the staircase, I couldn't believe how happy I felt. We found two good seats at the front edge of the balcony, just against the left wall. I sat down and continued to take in the architecture. We had a good view of the stage and the seats below were filling up. The tall brick walls on each side of the theater were softly lit by a row of large glass lampshades, facing up. I looked at the artistic detail of the ceiling. What once was grandiose, now seemed small and quaint.

The concert started, and it was good! The energy was high, the sound was loud and clear, and the lighting was perfect! I sat there on the edge of my chair, soaking it all in. The fans in the front, near the stage, stood through the whole show, singing every word with the band. As they played song after song, each word seemed to go straight into my heart. It felt like these songs were written specifically for me!

The stage lights seemed to dance with the music, casting colorful rays of red, yellow and purple across the gabled ceiling and down the brick walls. I was in heaven! I could not stop smiling, and I could not stop crying. Tears were pouring down my face but I didn't care. I felt hope. I felt a deep assurance that God was with me and He cared about me.

As I watched the lights dance down the wall, I noticed Stan's face turned towards mine. The band was playing their title song, "Where The Light Shines Through," and as I listened to the words of the song, I was wondering if maybe God would someday use my emotional scars for His glory. I turned to look at Stan, and he was smiling. The lights reflecting from the stage were dancing across his face, and his eyes were glistening. Maybe he felt the song was written for him too.

46

The Changes

I had made a commitment to keep a journal for one full year from April 11, 2016 to April 11, 2017. During that year I experienced new depths of sorrow but was also surprised by new heights of joy. In the early months, I felt like I was crawling through mud. Barely surviving each day. But by the time I turned the corner and headed into the last three months of that year, I felt like I was flying!

So much healing had happened in my mind and emotions. So much acceptance and forgiveness and surrender. I had no doubt that God cared for me and was guiding me into a life of freedom from fear. I began to believe that God intended good for me and He really did love me personally.

I wanted to share my story because I felt like there might be someone out there who needs to hear it. Maybe my story can give someone the courage to look up and cry out to God for His help. What God did for me, He can do for anyone!

Back in the early days of my journaling, my dear friend Gabby said, "Rose, sometimes God pulls us out of a bad situation so he can catapult us to the place He wants us to be." I indeed felt like I had been pulled out of my marriage, pulled

> *Maybe my story can give someone the courage to look up and cry out to God for His help.*

out of an abusive household, pulled away from a lying, unfaithful husband. But what I didn't expect was to be launched into a brand-new life!

Beautiful events were unfolding before my eyes. And my spirit, soul, and mind were being made healthy at such a fast rate that I could hardly contain my joy! My friends and family, and even my clients, were noticing the change in me, and they all seemed to share in my joy.

I noticed many different reactions by people around me. Those closest to me knew that the change was real and somehow spiritual. Even miraculous. They watched me go through the "valley of the shadow of death," and they were with me during the most painful times of heartbreak, acceptance, and surrender to God's sovereignty.

One time my stepmom, Abby, said, "Rose, I hardly recognize you. You've changed so much this year!"

I thought about that statement. It wasn't the first time I had heard it. I understood what she meant because there were times I didn't even recognize myself.

"I think you do recognize me, but you had forgotten what I was really like. Think about the younger version of me. The child me. Remember?"

"You're right!" she said, "It's like the real Rose is back!"

Sometimes I felt a little bit embarrassed about all the changes I had gone through. I felt shy about sharing with people that God rescued me out of an abusive marriage. I felt like people were judging me, and I felt like I had to give an answer to everyone for what had happened in my life over the last year. After a while I grew tired of trying to defend my actions. All I knew was God called out to me and exposed to me my husband's abusive treatment. All I cared about was that I knew God loved me and I knew that, in the end, He is the only One I need to answer to.

I had a note that I kept in my wallet. It was just three sentences long, but it gave me the courage to keep walking with my head held high. It was something Pastor Tim had said during one of his sermons a few months earlier. He was encouraging us to keep the faith, to stay the course, and to see ourselves as God sees us through what Jesus did for us on the cross.

"You gotta not care about what others think about you. You gotta not care about what you think about yourself. You gotta care about what God thinks about you!"

47

Blinders

I keep moving forward. Day by day. Sometimes moment by moment. I fill my schedule with plans so I'm not alone too much. I keep trusting God, knowing He is leading me. Tonight, I realized that it's hard to move forward when I keep wanting to glance back. I want to ponder what I've lost. I want to remember all the special times of my marriage to Frank, which is now over.

I have to trust God with what's behind me as much as I trust Him for what's before me. God can be my "rear-guard." Tonight, I offered a sweet sacrifice to God. I offered to give Him the "package of my past." I gave it to God and asked Him if He would hold it for me so I can function in the present. It's okay to cry when you offer a sacrifice.

They say that "you can't help but wonder." I say that you can and you should. I can't move forward if I'm always looking back. I prayed and asked God to give me spiritual horse blinders so I would stop trying to look for Frank or his girlfriend everywhere. I asked for blinders on my mind so I would stop being tempted to obsessively wonder where he was or how he was feeling or what he was doing or why he did what he did. I never understood why love lost is so hard for us humans. Why is it so tempting to drive past an ex's house? Morbid curiosity? I don't know why, and I don't care why. I just felt it was a very unhealthy behavior pattern, and I didn't want to get trapped in it.

The Lord answered my prayer quickly. One evening, as I was winding down for the night, I decided to scroll through Facebook and see what my friends and family were up to. I noticed the search icon on the top of the page, and I felt the urge to search Frank's page and then his girlfriend's page. I looked at that icon and felt a sick feeling in my stomach. I knew that if they had posted new pics, though it would ease my curiosity, it would probably make me feel sad or angry or sick.

I had prayed for God to give me spiritual blinders. I wanted to stop looking side to side. I wanted to stop looking back into my memories. I wanted to move forward, and I wanted to keep my eyes and mind facing forward. A clever idea popped into my head. I should search both of their names, then put a block on their pages to keep them from ever looking at my page.

I was happy with my idea. So I clicked through all the buttons to set up the block when a warning came up. "If you click 'accept' to this block, the person you are blocking will no longer be able to see your page, but you will also no longer be able to view their page." Interesting. I sat back and thought it about it for a moment. *If I set up this block, I will no longer be able to 'stalk' them via social media.* Hmm . . . essentially, I would be blocking myself from engaging in morbid curiosity and just plain unhealthy and unnecessary behavior. I clicked on the "accept" button and successfully blocked myself from ever spying on them again. Thank you, God, for helping me to put on healthy blinders.

After that, I turned off my phone and walked over to my journal. A poem came to me. The last time I had written a poem was over eleven years before. I was getting healthy in a way I would not have expected. When I finished writing the poem, I sat back in my chair and smiled. I liked the healing that was taking place in me. I felt proud of my new poem, and I felt proud for cooperating with what I felt the Lord was guiding me to do. I also felt relieved that I no longer had to try not to spy on Frank. I sealed the deal with the social media block.

"Locomotive"
by Rose Evans

You can't move forward
If you're always looking back
You're not a locomotive
Connected to some track
Take it, take it
I can't hold on to the past
You're before me
Come behind me
Sweet surrender at last
In the center of Your will
Time stands still

48

The Birthday Party

The last three months of my journal year flew by. It didn't take long for me to realize that God was bringing Stan and I together. I was falling in love, and I was not afraid. I was nervous, but I had given up fear. I felt comfortable knowing my eyes were firmly fixed on Jesus. I looked to Jesus above Stan, and I knew that Stan's heart was fixed on Jesus above me. I never understood the ways of love, and I used to be afraid of it. In my youth I avoided long-term serious relationships. I used to tell my brother Jared that "love was for poets." Now here I was, growing in grace, trusting God, and experiencing emotional healing. If love is for poets and God is love, then I am a poet!

Stan and I continued to sit together during every church service, and we continued going out for dinner dates. By mid-February, we were talking daily by phone, and I had even invited Stan to my apartment to have dinner with Charlie and me.

I was in constant contact with my mom by phone. I would call her at least once a week, and I would start the conversation with, "Well, do you want to hear the continuation of my life, which has become a sappy Hallmark love story?"

She would always reply, "Yes!" My mom is a hopeless romantic, always trusting in God's goodness and always looking for the best in people. She loves a good story, especially if there are twists in the plot. I think it made her heart happy to see me safe and healthy, and I think she was secretly pleased with how my story was turning out. She was the one who taught me that "All things work together for good for those that love God and are called according to His purposes" (Romans 8:28). And she also believed that "with God all things are possible" (Matthew 19:26b).

My mom came up to stay with us for the weekend to celebrate Charlie's twenty-third Birthday. My sister Leah came with her and brought her granddaughter Esther along. Leah and Esther stayed in a nearby hotel, while mom stayed with us. It was so much fun having my mom share my room with me for the weekend. Our apartment was now a lighthearted, happy place, filled with Charlie's friends coming and going, good food being shared around our big table, and lots of joyful conversation.

I was happy to share my joy with my mom. It was only a few months earlier that she had come up to spend a weekend with me to help me collect my items from storage. She was with me when I had to open up the boxes of my past and deal with the painful emotions of acceptance and release. She was with me as I lovingly set up my new apartment with Charlie, and it was my joy to now let her see "the goodness of God in the land of the living"!

Charlie's birthday party was so much fun! There was so much love and joy in the air. I invited Stan to come over, and my mom loved him immediately. I believe the feeling was mutual. My big sister Leah also felt comfortable with Stan right away. It was as if she was reunited with a long-lost brother. She wasted no time chatting with him about their similar taste in the Christian music artists of the seventies and eighties.

Winter was on its way out, and the branches were beginning to bud on my beloved trees that lined the front lawn below my bedroom window. The evening sun was streaming into the apartment as everyone happily chatted away while my mom and I finished making Charlie's birthday cake.

At one point I was so overwhelmed by the joy that I had to step outside to be alone for a moment. I walked out the front door and down the steps to the front lawn. I could still hear the laughter and voices of those I loved filling the small space of my upstairs apartment. Everything was good. Everyone was happy, and my heart was full of joy.

I couldn't help but think of the Lord. His presence felt so close to me during the hard times. Would He stay close to me even in the good times? I stood downstairs, looking up towards my bedroom window. I started humming a song. It was a U2 song, of course, and I just stood there for a few minutes, humming and smiling and listening to the sound of happiness coming from my apartment.

The song I was humming was "All I Want Is You," and as I stood there for a moment, I started to sing the words out loud. I was thinking about how much I loved my son and how much I loved my mom and my family. I thought about how much I was beginning to love Stan, and then I thought about how much I loved the Lord.

As I finished singing the song, I heard myself singing the last part out loud and quite passionately. "All I want is You!!!" And as tears began to well up in my eyes, I realized that above everything else in life, what I want more than anything is God's love.

I smiled and drew in a deep breath. *It's okay to be happy. It's okay to feel so much love for people that it feels like your heart might explode for joy! And it's okay to desire that your deepest love remain reserved for your highest love. It's okay to love God the most.*

As I walked back into the apartment, Esther asked where I had been. I told her I felt overwhelmed by so much love that I had to go outside to pray for a minute.

She asked, "Are you sure that you and Stan are 'just friends'?" She is very clever for a ten-year-old and very observant.

I smiled at her and said, "Well, I do like Stan very much!"

She smiled back with the contentment that she was somehow in on a new secret. She said, "Rose, your eyes look like the ocean!"

I smiled at her sweet face and said, "My heart is happy!"

I will never forget that night. Our time living in the apartment would be remembered as one of the happiest times of our life. I have a photographic memory imprinted on my heart of Charlie's smiling face as we all sang "Happy Birthday" to him. His eyes were sparkling as he looked around the room at each of us. The glow from the twenty-three candles on his cake seemed to dance across his face. He looked happy and very content. These were good times! God was bringing "beauty from ashes, the oil of joy for sorrow. The garment of praise for the spirit of heaviness" (Isaiah 61:3b).

Charlie made a wish and blew out the candles and laughed as everyone cheered and applauded. He smiled and said to me quietly, "This has been my best birthday ever!"

49

The Sapphire

Spring was in full bloom, and I was well into the last quarter of my commitment to keep a journal for one year. It was around eight o'clock on the evening of March 1 that I heard a gentle knock on the front door of my apartment. I knew who it was. Stan had just called and asked if he could stop by my apartment for a minute. He had something very important to ask me.

I jumped up from my desk and quietly walked to the front door. Charlie had fallen asleep in the living room while watching a movie, and I didn't want to wake him. I opened the front door, and there stood Stan! I could see his face clearly from the glow of my porch light. He was smiling, and his eyes were looking intently into mine.

I whispered, "Come in!" As he stepped into my entryway, I whispered, "Charlie fell asleep watching a movie. Wait here." Then I tiptoed into the living room to see if Charlie was still asleep, and he was. I walked back to Stan and said, "Hold on." I could see that in his right hand, he was holding a small white box with a black satin ribbon tied around it. The ribbon was tied into a neat bow, which rested on the top of the small box. In his other hand, he had something in a brown paper bag.

Stan just stood there in the entryway smiling at me as I frantically bounced around the apartment. I tiptoed back into the living room and into the kitchen and then back into the entryway. I knew what Stan was here for, and I was excited! Stan had something important to ask me, and I couldn't find a place in my small apartment to invite him into.

Just then a peace came over me. I wasn't afraid; I was excited! I knew God was bringing Stan and I together, so I just decided to calm down and enjoy this beautiful moment. I walked back to Stan, who hadn't moved from the entryway. He was still smiling. I said, "I'm sorry. I'm just super excited, and I don't know where to have you come in. Charlie is asleep in the living room." I looked again at the packages in his hands and said, "May I take that bag and put it in the kitchen for you?"

He looked down at the bag and handed it to me. "Oh yes, that would be great. Thank you."

He followed me into the kitchen, and we peeked over at Charlie. It seemed funny to me that Charlie had fallen to sleep at eight o'clock, but it was also nice to be able to have a private moment with Stan. I turned to Stan and said, "I see that you have an important question to ask me. Would you mind asking me in my bedroom? We can come back into the kitchen after that to see what's in that bag if you'd like."

Stan smiled and said, "Yes, Rose, that would be fine."

I took Stan's hand and walked him to my bedroom, which was just past the apartment entryway. My room was neat and clean, so I just sat on the edge of my bed and said to Stan, "What is it, my love?"

Stan knelt down in front of where I was sitting and took both of my hands and said, "Rose, will you please be my wife?"

I smiled and felt a joy coming up from deep down inside. I felt shy and quickly said, "Of course!"

Stan smiled, kissed me, and said, "Thank you!" Then he opened up the small box.

I looked inside and started to cry. It was the most beautiful sapphire ring I had ever seen! The ring had three large sapphires set on a band of white gold. And each sapphire was surrounded by sparkling diamonds. I put the ring on my left ring finger and just stared at it. It looked like a jewel that should be worn by a princess. My thoughts went back to the puzzling dream I had written about earlier in the journal. I had dreamed that someone gave me a sapphire ring, and at the time I would have never imagined it was going to be an engagement ring! I smiled at Stan and said, "Thank you!"

Then I leaned forward and asked Stan if he wouldn't

mind waiting in my room for a few minutes. I wanted to wake Charlie and tell him the news before anyone else. I walked into the living room and glanced at the beautiful ring that was now on my finger. I was smiling and at total peace. I knelt beside the couch and gently shook Charlie's shoulder. He opened his eyes and started to sit up. The living room was dark but comfortable. Light was coming in from the kitchen, and a soft glow fell on Charlie's face from the movie on the television that no one was watching.

"Charlie, I have something very special to tell you, and I wanted you to know before anyone else." Charlie sat further up on the sofa and rubbed his eyes and smiled. "Stan is here," I said, "and he has asked me to marry him. Look!" I said, as I held up my hand to show him the ring.

Charlie looked at the ring and then back at me smiling. "Oh, wow! That's awesome!" he said. "Congratulations!"

I walked back into my bedroom where Stan was now sitting on the edge of my bed. I thanked him for waiting for me and asked if he would like to come into the kitchen with me. We were met by Charlie as we all headed into the kitchen. Charlie looked at Stan with a big smile on his face.

"Congratulations!" he said to Stan, as he held out his hand for a handshake.

Stan received his handshake and pulled him in for a hug. "Thank you, Charlie," he said.

Stan opened up the small paper bag and pulled out a bottle of expensive scotch. "I picked this up on the way over, hoping that your mom would say yes," Stan told Charlie.

"Oh, wow!" I said. "I don't even know if I like scotch, but I do think that the three of us should have a toast together."

I pulled down three glasses from the cupboard, and Stan poured a small amount of scotch into each glass. I handed one of the glasses to Charlie and said, "Would you please say a toast to us?"

Charlie smiled and said, "Um, okay." The kitchen was cozy. There was a comfortable glow on our faces. It was more than just good lighting. We were happy. As we stood there together, holding our glasses up, Charlie said, "Here's to happiness, to healing and . . ."

As Charlie paused to find the last words for his toast, I said, "To love?"

"Yes!" Charlie said. "To love."

JOURNAL ENTRY: 3/2/17

In the early days of keeping this journal, my mom said, "This sounds like a pat answer, but the truth is that 'this too shall pass.'" It's true. Healing in our lives is possible. None of us get through this journey without pain. For me, I have decided to live the rest of my life in total surrender to God.

Pain and grief happen in life. All sorts of bad things can happen. But God can also happen if you let Him. I still go through each day moment by moment sometimes, but I choose love. I choose health. I choose forgiveness. I choose to trust God.

God comforts me while I sleep, and He teaches my soul to trust Him. I have been patient in my affliction, and I am blessed with perfect peace. My God has become my champion!

CHAPTER

Final Journal Entries

As I draw near to the ending of this journal, my spirit feels sad. Nostalgic almost. I would not want to go through any of it again, except for the closeness I have experienced with God. From the time that I sensed Him calling to me until now, I am amazed by His goodness and His love.

It is a guarantee that there will be hard times in life. It's part of the journey. What I went through this last year was very, very difficult. Impossible at times. My courage comes from knowing God is with me and He loves me.

This morning I read a sweet verse in the Bible.

"The Lord is close to the brokenhearted and saves those who are crushed in spirit." —Psalm 34:18

"I have been crucified with Christ and I no longer live but Christ lives in me. The life I now live, I live by faith in the Son of God, who loved me and gave Himself for me." — Galatians 2:20

"This one thing I do; forgetting what is behind and straining toward what is ahead, I press on toward the goal to win the prize for which God has called me heavenward in Christ Jesus." — Philippians 3:13b-14

"You will go out in joy and be led forth in peace; the mountains and hills will burst into song before you, and all the trees of the field will clap their hands." —Isaiah 55:12

Dear God, your grace is all I've ever needed. If I just allow you, you will write my story. You are the best Author, and you are the Finisher of our faith. All that we have comes from You. My

God!! Your grace is sufficient for me, and your love is more than I could ever contain, this side of heaven. Thank you. I love you.

"When hard pressed, I cried to the Lord; He brought me into a spacious place. The Lord is with me; I will not be afraid. What can mere mortals do to me?"

—Psalm 118:5,6

THE END

Afterword

Stan and Rose married on "May Day," 5/1/17, surrounded by the smiling faces of their children in the middle of a beautiful park. The trees were in full bloom, exploding in the colors of spring. There was no fear, only excitement and joy, as they exchanged their vows to one another before the justice of the peace.

Rose continues to grow in grace, always looking forward, while trusting Jesus with what lies behind. She has progressed with her ability to play her guitar, to which she owes Stan a great deal of gratitude. He is a patient teacher.

When Stan and Rose are not busy with work and church ministry, they enjoy taking long walks through the woods or city streets, happily discussing their hopes and dreams. They are blessed to be enjoying "the goodness of God in the land of the living."

We don't know the plans God has for us, but He does. Every person has their own story, but the theme of God's story is true for everyone. His plans for you are good.

> *The theme of God's story is true for everyone. His plans for you are good.*

"Trust in the Lord with all your heart and lean not on your own understanding; in all your ways submit to him, and he will make your paths straight."

—Proverbs 3:5 (NIV)

"For I know the plans I have for you, declares the Lord, plans for welfare and not for evil, to give you a future and a hope."

—Jeremiah 29:11 (ESV)

"It's Beautiful"
A Poem by Jeanne Jensen

Do you know what it's like
To walk in a miracle
Do you know how it feels
To be stopped in your tracks

Do you know what it's like
To have longings fulfilled
To be put back together
With gold in the cracks

Do you know what it's like
It's the tail of a star
Drawing close to the One
Who once felt so far

The light that's shining on me
Is so much more than sunlight
No fear
He's near
In my tear
Are the colors of the rainbow

About the Author

Jeanne Jensen was born in Southern California where she was raised in a Christian home. At a young age, she loved to write poetry and song lyrics and later graduated into writing short skits and plays for her church. Many years later, after going through the harrowing experience detailed in this book, she felt obliged to pick up her pen once again to tell her story.

When not writing, Jeanne enjoys playing her guitar and creating music with her husband Peter. They are both actively involved in their church as part of the worship team and serving in the youth and children's ministries.

Always up for an adventure, Jeanne loves a good road trip—especially when the road leads to spending time with their combined children and grandchildren!

The little book of
BIG
WEIGHTLOSS™

by Bernadette Fisers

for my daughter Lilli
may she never have the weight problems i've had

LONDO

014186939 6

TRANSWORLD PUBLISHERS
61–63 Uxbridge Road, London W5 5SA
www.penguin.co.uk

Transworld is part of the Penguin Random House group of companies
whose addresses can be found at global.penguinrandomhouse.com

First published by Bernadette Fisers, 2016
This revised edition published by Penguin Random House Australia Pty Ltd, 2017
First published in Great Britain in 2017 by Bantam Press, an imprint of Transworld Publishers

Layout and graphic art: Myrtle Jeffs
Photography: Terence Langendoen
Images courtesy Leremy/Shutterstock

A CIP catalogue record for this book is available from the British Library.

ISBN 9780593079423

Printed and bound in Italy by Printer Trento

Penguin Random House is committed to a sustainable future for our business, our readers and our planet.
This book is made from Forest Stewardship Council® certified paper.

1 3 5 7 9 10 8 6 4 2